"In their penetrating account of Marx's famous hatchet job on the nineteenth-century left, Hudis and Anderson go to the heart of issues haunting the left in the twenty-first century: what would a society look like without work, wages, GDP growth and human self-oppression."
—Paul Mason, writer for *New Statesman* and author of *Postcapitalism: A Guide to Our Future*

"This is a compelling moment for a return to Marx's most visionary writings. Among those is his often-neglected *Critique of the Gotha Program.* In this exciting new translation, we can hear Marx urging socialists of his day to remain committed to a truly radical break with capitalism. And in Peter Hudis's illuminating introductory essay we are reminded that Marx's vision of a society beyond capitalism was democratic and emancipatory to its very core. This book is a major addition to the anticapitalist library."
—David McNally, Cullen Distinguished Professor of History, University of Houston, and author of *Monsters of the Market*

"*Critique of the Gotha Program* is a key text for understanding Marx's vision of an emancipated society beyond capitalism. With an excellent introduction by Peter Hudis, this new translation is both timely and important. Returning to Marx's pathbreaking essay can give new direction to the political struggles of our time."
—Martin Hägglund, Birgit Baldwin Professor of Comparative Literature and Humanities, Yale University, author of *This Life*

"This new edition of Marx's *Critique of the Gotha Program*, with an illuminating introduction by Peter Hudis, confirms that to re-translate is not only to re-animate old questions in the body of new words, but is also to propel writing towards contemporary exigencies. Arcing across times, the then of a first articulation connects to the now of hindsight and to the unwritten terms of an open future. While the delusions of real existing state socialism have dispelled, confusions around the role of the state in an emancipating society persist. In this short metatext, Marx's snappish commentaries and his forensic dissections of weasel words and hollow phrases reveal how language matters, because it conveys and betrays ideology, policy, and underlying standpoints. Translation works with this malleability of language. Meaning turns on a dime: political orientation can be realigned, if the slogan evinces exactitude, acknowledging history and horizons of possibility. We should learn, through this book, to read closer, better, and in dialogue."

—Esther Leslie, professor of political aesthetics, Birkbeck College, University of London, and author of *Walter Benjamin*

"This new translation of Marx's *Critique of the Gotha Program* includes an introductory essay by Peter Hudis, which points to Marx's distinction between value, that is, the socially necessary time required to produce a commodity, and labor itself, that is, the actual number of hours a worker engages in. He provides a provocative and useful critique of Lenin's conception of the transition to socialism, and of subsequent Marxist-Leninist and social democratic conceptions of a socialist society. This raises questions about the nature of both labor and value in a society in which both have been transformed by technology. Nevertheless Hudis's analysis provides a clarifying and useful critique of both social democratic and Marxist-Leninist conceptions of socialism/communism."
—Barbara Epstein, professor in the History of Consciousness Department, University of California, Santa Cruz, and author of *Political Power and Cultural Revolution*

"*Critique of the Gotha Program* is one of Marx's great strategic texts, often cited but little read. At a time when the questions of transition and of the forms of organization to exit capitalism are so urgent, this new edition should be saluted. Elaborated by the Marxist-Humanist tendency, it makes a valuable contribution, thanks to the way it situates Marx's *Critique* in historical perspective."
—Isabelle Garo, editing committee, *Grande Édition des Oeuvres de Marx et Engels*, Paris

 **◼SPECTRE▶**

Editor: Sasha Lilley

Spectre is a series of penetrating and indispensable works of, and about, radical political economy. Spectre lays bare the dark underbelly of politics and economics, publishing outstanding and contrarian perspectives on the maelstrom of capital—and emancipatory alternatives—in crisis. The companion Spectre Classics imprint unearths essential works of radical history, political economy, theory and practice, to illuminate the present with brilliant, yet unjustly neglected, ideas from the past.

Spectre

Greg Albo, Sam Gindin, and Leo Panitch, *In and Out of Crisis: The Global Financial Meltdown and Left Alternatives*

David McNally, *Global Slump: The Economics and Politics of Crisis and Resistance*

Sasha Lilley, *Capital and Its Discontents: Conversations with Radical Thinkers in a Time of Tumult*

Sasha Lilley, David McNally, Eddie Yuen, and James Davis, *Catastrophism: The Apocalyptic Politics of Collapse and Rebirth*

Peter Linebaugh, *Stop, Thief! The Commons, Enclosures, and Resistance*

Peter Linebaugh, *The Incomplete, True, Authentic, and Wonderful History of May Day*

Richard A. Walker, *Pictures of a Gone City: Tech and the Dark Side of Prosperity in the San Francisco Bay Area*

Silvia Federici, *Patriarchy of the Wage: Notes on Marx, Gender, and Feminism*

Raymond B. Craib, *Adventure Capitalism: A History of Libertarian Exit, from the Era of Decolonization to the Digital Age*

Spectre Classics

E.P. Thompson, *William Morris: Romantic to Revolutionary*

Victor Serge, *Men in Prison*

Victor Serge, *Birth of Our Power*

Karl Marx, *Critique of the Gotha Program*

Critique of the Gotha Program

Karl Marx

With a new introduction by Peter Hudis

Translated and annotated by
Kevin B. Anderson and Karel Ludenhoff

SPECTRE
CLASSICS

PM

Critique of the Gotha Program
Karl Marx
With a new introduction by Peter Hudis
Translated and annotated by Kevin B. Anderson and Karel Ludenhoff
This edition © PM Press 2023

ISBN: 978–1–62963–916–1 (paperback)
ISBN: 978–1–62963–926–0 (ebook)

Library of Congress Control Number: 2021936594

Cover by John Yates / www.stealworks.com
Interior design by briandesign

10 9 8 7 6 5 4 3 2 1

PM Press
PO Box 23912
Oakland, CA 94623
www.pmpress.org

Printed in the USA

In memory of James Obst
aka Jim Mills, J. Turk
(1953–2020),
friend, comrade, revolutionary

Contents

ACKNOWLEDGMENTS   xi

INTRODUCTION The Alternative to Capitalism in Marx's
Critique of the Gotha Program by Peter Hudis   1

Program of the Socialist Workers' Party of Germany
[Gotha Program]   43

Letter by Karl Marx to Wilhelm Bracke   47

Critique of the Gotha Program   51

Afterword by Peter Linebaugh   79

INDEX   95

ABOUT THE CONTRIBUTORS   99

Acknowledgments

The final versions of Peter Hudis's introduction, the new translation of Marx's *Critique of the Gotha Program,* and that of the Gotha Program itself are the result of several years of discussion, in which numerous members and friends of the International Marxist-Humanist Organization participated. We are grateful for all their comments and suggestions.

The Alternative to Capitalism in Marx's *Critique of the Gotha Program*

By Peter Hudis

I

Today, we face a serious crisis.[1] By "we" I mean those seeking to challenge and overcome capitalism. By "crisis" I mean not only today's severe political and economic retrogression but also the lack of an *adequate* conception of our goal—a noncapitalist society—that can give action its direction.

We need theoretical as well as practical sources to confront and deal with this crisis. An especially vital one is Karl Marx's 1875 *Critique of the Gotha Program*. It was written with a crisis very much in mind—one not that much different from our own.

In 1875, for the first time, the two main wings of German socialism—the followers of Marx (known as Eisenachers) and of Ferdinand Lassalle (founder of the first independent working-class party in Germany)—became a single organization at a unity congress in the city of Gotha. It was supposed to herald a new beginning in the struggle against capitalism. Indeed, the new organization rapidly grew after 1875; by 1905 its successor, the German Social-Democratic Party (SPD) was the most powerful socialist organization on earth, with over a million members. But the new beginning was not to be. Marx saw the unity congress as a tragic error, because it was bought at too high a price: a capitulation to the doctrines of Lassalle, whom Marx had denounced years earlier as "a future workers' dictator." At first he threatened to cut off all relations with the new party; though he decided not to, within a few years he concluded it would be better if the united organization (now widely heralded as "Marxist") ceased to exist.[2] The reason for Marx's dissatisfaction becomes clear from the *Critique of the Gotha Program*. It was unpublished in his lifetime and first reached the light of day in 1891—only to then be dutifully ignored. His own followers, he realized, suffered from an extremely defective conception of the alternative to capitalism.

The past one hundred years is the history of a series of defective conceptions of an alternative to capitalism put into practice. The result has been one failure and halfway house after another. Neither the reformist social democratic version of socialism nor its revolutionary variant that was taken over by various forms of Stalinism and Marxist-Leninism succeeded in posing a viable alternative; instead, each morphed into some version of capitalism. Nor did the anarchists fill this void in developing an alternative, since their correct emphasis on democratic and nonstatist forms of decision-making largely failed to consider that the capitalist law of value can exist even under conditions of cooperative or collective production. History, of course, does not come to an end because of the limitations of radical currents. New passions and forces for liberation continuously arise, posing new questions and challenges of their own. This is especially seen in the array of new social movements and freedom struggles in recent years, by women, Blacks, Latinx, and other oppressed peoples, and of LGBTQ movements. Many in these struggles are reaching for a vision of a new society that transcends the limits of both existing capitalism and the so-called socialist and communist regimes of the past. Yet too few theorists and activists are working to provide such a vision. Herein lies our crisis: just when we need an alternative that can speak to masses of people the most, we possess it the least.

We clearly need a new beginning. But a beginning needs a proper foundation. Where is it to be found? For several years, those associated with the Marxist-Humanist current founded in the US by Raya Dunayevskaya have sought to respond to this question. This publication is part of an invitation to rethink the nature of capitalism and the alternative to it, by encountering anew the work in which Marx most fully discussed the nature of socialist or communist society: his *Critique of the Gotha Program*.

We are aware that we can't live by the truths of a different era. We face problems that Marx didn't envision or face. But we are also aware that no thinker developed a more far-reaching and *dialectical* critique of capitalism. This is because a positive vision of the future was immanent in his negative critique.

We are preparing this new and revised translation of the *Critique of the Gotha Program* on the 150th anniversary of the Paris Commune of 1871, one of the most creative efforts to forge an alternative to capitalism. It has never been more urgent to create a viable alternative to existing society. This book is a contribution to the ongoing effort to develop a philosophically grounded alternative to capitalism, and we hope you will join this endeavor.

II

The Gotha Program is brief—about 630 words. Marx's critique of it is more than ten times as long. Each word was subjected to relentless analysis and criticism. His *Critique* was intended as marginal notes—not as a self-contained essay. It is not a systematic treatise but an outline of some basic concepts. The *Critique of the Gotha Program* does not therefore provide an *answer* as to what society could be like after capitalism. But it provides *ground* for getting there, since it presents concepts that pinpoint the specific social relations that are needed in order to uproot capitalism.

The Gotha Program resulted from a series of developments in the German socialist movement. In 1863 the first truly independent working-class socialist party in Germany was established by Ferdinand Lassalle—the Allgemeiner Deutscher Arbeiterverein (General Union of German Workers, or ADAV). Over the course of the next decade it grew rapidly, winning almost two hundred thousand votes in the parliamentary elections of 1874. While for a number of years Lassalle collaborated with Marx (then living in exile in London), by 1862 Marx broke off relations with him over a series of political and theoretical disagreements, the most significant being Lassalle's effort to form an alliance with Prussian autocrat Bismarck in order to secure social reforms.

At the time, Marx had very few followers in Germany—and the ones he had, such as Wilhelm Liebknecht, had originally been members of Lassalle's ADAV. Nevertheless, in 1869—two years after the publication of Volume I of *Capital*—an alliance of socialists linked to Marx, and grouped around Liebknecht and August Bebel, founded the Sozialdemokratische Arbeiterpartei (Social Democratic Workers' Party, or SDAP) at Eisenach (henceforth known as "Eisenachers"). Operating independently of the ADAV, it rapidly grew in size and was almost as large as the ADAV by 1874. While Marx was often credited—or condemned—for controlling the SDAP from behind the scenes, he was deeply immersed in the work in the First International during the late 1860s and early 1870s and therefore did not play a direct role in the SDAP.[3]

In 1875 Bebel and Liebknecht entered into negotiations with the ADAV (Lassalle had died in 1864) with the aim of creating a unified party—without so much as informing Marx and Engels. When the program of the new party was published shortly thereafter—called the Sozialistische Arbeiterpartei Deutschlands (Socialist Workers' Party of Germany, or SAPD)—Marx and Engels were furious. They considered it a betrayal of the principles of revolutionary socialism and a capitulation to Lassalleanism.

Two points should be kept in mind before turning to Marx's *Critique*. First, its discussion of the new society is consistent with earlier treatments in *The Poverty of Philosophy*, the *Grundrisse*, *Capital*, and other writings.[4] Marx largely avoided entering into discussions of a future society on the grounds that communism is not a utopian ideal that one tries to impose *upon* the masses but is instead the result of the self-activity *of* the masses. He admired many utopian thinkers (especially Charles Fourier and Robert Owen) for their insights into the exploitative nature of the capitalist mode of production, but he also criticized their lack of engagement with the actual social force that could bring their ideals to realization—the proletariat. For Marx, a fundamental problem with capitalism is that it robs individuals of their agency by treating them as *things*, as mere sources of economic value.

Hence, engaging in abstract speculation of how the world "ought" to be, irrespective of the actual struggles of the oppressed, fails to challenge capitalism's denial of the right of those it oppresses and exploits to shape their own destiny. The alternative to capitalism, he held, has to emerge from *within* capitalism, from the struggles of oppressed people to redefine themselves in the face of the dehumanization that characterizes modern society.

At the same time, the widespread assumption that Marx had little or nothing to say about a new society is misplaced. His critique of capital, developed by listening to the voices of the oppressed, is not a mere empirical description of existing conditions; it is a *dialectical* analysis that intimates the forms of life that can emerge from efforts to uproot them. A dialectical analysis grasps the object of investigation in its *process of becoming*, the tendencies within a given phenomenon that compel it to change and even to transform into its opposite. Since Marx aimed to show that capitalism is not an immutable part of human existence but a transitory phenomenon that "under penalty of death" must give way to a higher social order, he could not help but discuss aspects of a new society—much as he disavowed any utopian effort to create "blueprints for the future."

What especially led Marx to discuss a future society at times was his battle of ideas with rival left-wing tendencies. Marx did not create the idea of socialism or communism; at the end of 1843 he joined an existing communist movement that long preceded him. This movement contained a multitude of tendencies, each with their own understanding of capitalism and the alternative to it. Marx critically engaged them, pointing out their accomplishments and pitfalls—whether it be Proudhon, Weitling, Bakunin, or Lassalle. Some of Marx's most explicit discussions of a future postcapitalist society were penned in such critiques, especially as seen in *The Poverty of Philosophy*, the *Grundrisse*, and *Critique of the Gotha Program*. Just a few years before writing the latter was the historical turning point of the Paris Commune of 1871. It was the first time that the working class seized power on its own behalf and moved to reorganize society. The task now became for socialists to absorb and take off from this turning point. When he saw that the Gotha Program was a regression from the high point reached with the Paris Commune, he could no longer avoid entering into a more detailed discussion of the alternative to capitalism.

Second, the 1875 *Critique* is integral to Marx's critique of capital. For Marx, a proper understanding of the alternative to a society dominated by capital lies in grasping the nature of capital. This is not easy, since capital is a mystifying phenomenon. Is it a thing such as a machine? Or is it intangible, like money? Is it a social relation, and if so, of what sort? Marx spent three decades trying to answer such questions. It was a never-ending, unfinished process; he spent several years after the Paris Commune revising Volume I of *Capital* in order to improve its analysis in light of it. But what shocked him was that just when a new and revised French edition of *Capital* came off the press in 1875, his own followers were ignoring his theoretical insights in favor of Lassalle's. Because they lacked an adequate understanding of capital, they also had an inadequate understanding of the alternative to capital. It is no accident that when Marx sent his *Critique of the Gotha Program* to the leaders of the newly formed SAPD, he included with it copies of the French edition of *Capital*.

Marx's great achievement in *Capital* is showing that capital is self-expanding value, and capitalism's defining feature is that labor assumes a value-*form*. Value, or wealth measured in money, is the product of a specific form of labor—abstract or homogeneous labor. But what exactly does this *mean*? It is often said that "labor is the source of all value." The more hours of labor embodied in a product, the greater its economic value. But when we look at this more closely, it becomes clear that this cannot be the case. If "labor" as such were the source of value, we would to be told to work as slowly as possible—since the greater the number of hours expended in producing a product, the greater its value. But this clearly never happens. This is because the value of a commodity is determined not by the *actual* amount of time taken to produce it but by the *socially necessary labor time* established on a global level. This average varies continuously due to technological innovations that increase the productivity of labor. Concrete labor—the varied kinds of labor employed in making use values—becomes increasingly dominated by abstract labor, or labor that is governed by the dictates of socially average necessary labor time. Abstract labor is the *substance* of value, while socially necessary labor time is the *measure* of value. If you make a product in excess of the average amount of time established by the world market, the extra time does not create value—and so you are told to work harder and faster. If you make a product in less time than the social average, employers will try to get other workers to do the same, forcing them to work harder and faster. Capitalism continuously looks for ways to get more value out of fewer hours of labor, by appropriating ever more surplus labor time.

Value may be a rather *abstract* category, insofar as it is not *visible* but is a *real* entity that depends upon a very real kind of human activity: *labor that is constrained by an abstract time determination outside of the workers' control.*[5] This is the basis of capitalist class exploitation, its destruction of nature, and its depersonalization of human relations. Marx's critique of value production is integral to the *humanism* that defines his entire theoretical and political project.

The issue of *time* is fundamental to the way we strive to live our lives. Our time is finite and limited. *Consciousness* of time pervades all facets of human existence and governs so much of who we are and what we do. Are we in control of our limited time? Or does a force independent of us control our time? How can we claim to be "free" if the latter is the case? The central and decisive argument that Marx makes against capitalism is that we are not in control of time: on the contrary, time increasingly controls us. Time takes on the form of a rigid, albeit invisible, force that confronts us as a person apart—and it does so in the form of socially necessary labor time, an abstract average that determines the "value" or monetary worth of our labor that we must submit to, regardless of our needs and desires. The way in which time imposes itself upon us as an autonomous force to which we must succumb is unique to capitalism. Therefore, the only way to exit from capitalism is to put an end to its tyranny.

Marxists have traditionally emphasized private ownership of the means of production and a "free market" as the main problem of capitalism. Marx surely opposed both. However, primarily focusing on them obscures the way our lived time is subjected to an abstract time determination outside of our control. This blind spot has led many to equate "socialism" or "communism" with nationalized property and a planned economy. But as events of the past hundred years show, such a narrow conception does not provide a viable alternative to capitalism. Radical movements have suffered from the *depth* of Marx's critique of capital not being fully understood.

In the famous section of *Capital* on the fetishism of commodities, Marx wrote that human relations *necessarily* take on the form of relations between things so long as they are governed by the dictates of value production. So total is this dehumanization that social agents come to perceive it as natural and normal. This explains why it has been so hard to develop an alternative to capitalism. As production for the sake of augmenting value colonizes ever more dimensions of the life-world, it increasingly appears to be an immutable fact of human existence. Not just apologists for the system but also those opposed to it readily fall prey to this fetishism.

Marx states that this mental constraint begins to dissolve only when we encounter "other forms of production."[6] He first turns to the *past* by surveying precapitalist economic forms in which "*directly* social labor" prevails instead of the indirectly social labor that characterizes value production. Under feudalism, for example, relations of personal dependence predominate, in which "there is no need for labors and their products to assume a fantastic form different from their reality."[7] No abstract medium, such as exchange value, mediates human relations. Hence, production that augments value as an end in itself is specific to capitalism and capitalism alone. He then turns to the *future*, writing: "Let us finally imagine, for a change, an association of free human beings [*Menschen*], working with the means of production held in common."[8] This does not refer to a formal transfer of private property to collective or state entities. Transferring property deeds is a *juridical* action, which does not end class domination. Marx refers to "free human beings" owning the means of production, which means they exert effective and not just nominal control over the labor process. *And that is not possible unless the producers democratically control the labor process through their own self-activity.*

He goes on to state that in a postcapitalist society, products are "directly objects of utility" and do not assume a value form. Exchange value and universalized commodity production come to an end. Producers decide how to make, distribute, and consume the total social product. One part is used to renew the means of production; the other "is consumed by members of the association as means of subsistence."[9] He invokes neither the market nor the state as the medium by which this is achieved. He instead envisions a planned distribution of labor time by individuals who are no longer subjected to socially necessary labor time. Abstract labor is abolished, since a *concretum—actual* labor time— becomes a measure of social relations instead of an abstract average that individuals do not control. Socially necessary labor time confronts individuals as a person apart, irrespective of their sensuous and spiritual needs, whereas actual labor time is the material and mental activity of individuals mediating their relations with nature. Distributing the elements of production on the basis of actual labor time represents a radical break from capitalism, since it signals the abolition of its peculiar form of labor—*abstract* labor. This *form* of organizing *time* is the cardinal principle of Marx's concept of communism and serves as the basis of his further outline of a new society in the *Critique of the Gotha Program*.

III

What is *new* with the *Critique*, even as compared with Marx's earlier work, is that it explicitly distinguishes between a lower and higher phase of communism and discusses the new society in an *organizational* context, in attacking his own followers for capitulating to the ideas of Ferdinand Lassalle.

Marx begins his critique by taking issue with the Gotha Program's conflation of material wealth with economic value.

He does so from two directions. He first critiques its statement that "labor is *the source* of all wealth" on the grounds that "*Nature* is just as much the source of use values." This is no mere hair-splitting. The idea that labor is the source of material wealth renders invisible humanity's dependence on nature. Moreover, it treats value, or wealth that takes a monetary expression, as a transhistorical reality instead of as the governing principle of *capitalism*. Material wealth is (in part) a product of nature, whereas value is *socially constructed*. By conflating these two, the Gotha Program "falsely ascribes *supernatural creative power* to labor" by presuming that value production is a natural property of laboring. But if that is the case, it follows that the "peculiar social character of the labor"[10] that serves as the substance of value (abstract labor) is a permanent condition of life that can never be altered.

Marx continues his critique of the conflation of material wealth and value by taking issue with the Gotha Program's declaration that "the proceeds of labor belong undiminished with equal right to all members of society." This suggests that in socialism the producers receive as much wealth from society as they produce for it. Marx counters that a portion of wealth will always need to be set aside to provide for children, adults who cannot work, education, and to replenish the means of production. He finds it absurd to promise producers that they will receive the full fruits of their labor. The program does so because it conflates wealth with value. It is no secret that in capitalism, workers create more value than they receive in wages and benefits; the remainder is surplus value, part of which becomes profit. By failing to make the analytical distinction between wealth and value, the Gotha Program assumes that abolishing surplus value requires giving individual workers the full fruits of their labor—even though this is clearly a completely imprac-tical perspective.

This is of critical importance, since many today assume that socialism is defined by a "fair" redistribution of income and resources. Given the extreme social and economic inequality of contemporary society, the demand for a fairer redistribution of surplus value is understandable. But it is impossible to redistribute what does not *exist*. A project defined by the redistribution of surplus value presumes the continued existence of value production. Since "value can be formally defined as *the abstract and reified form of social labor*,"[11] calls to *redistribute* instead of *abolish* value leave unaddressed the need to uproot the alienated forms of labor and everyday life that are central to capitalism. This defines the failed approach of all social democratic, Stalinist, and market socialist variants of distributive economics: since they assume that value production exists even under "socialism," they fail to challenge the alienated human relations that constitute its substance. *Humanism*, at least in Marx's sense of the word, vanishes from view.

Two other issues deeply troubled Marx about the Gotha Program—its endorsement of Lassalle's theory of the "iron law of wages" and its capitulation to nationalism in saying "Not a word ... *about the international functions* of the German working class!"

The "iron law of wages" held that in capitalism wages tend toward the minimum required to sustain the laborer: wages can never drop below subsistence, since that would threaten the physical existence of the worker, but neither can they rise much above subsistence, given competition among workers for employment. While Marx is often associated with this idea (often referred to as "the absolute immiseration of the working class"), he repeatedly attacked it as a vulgar application of Malthus's theory of population. Lassalle held that since increases in wages lead workers to marry earlier and have more children, the supply of labor ends up outstripping demand—resulting in a decline in wages. The logical conclusion is that the efforts of trade unions to secure higher wages for its members are bound to be ultimately fruitless.[12] Marx was especially infuriated that this would be included in the program, since the Eisenachers had long been active in trade unions, in contrast to the ADAV—indeed, it was a big reason for the growth of the SDAP in the early and mid-1870s. Including such language threatened to cut the party off from an important section of the working class.

What may seem like debate over an obscure theoretical issue was really about whether a revolutionary party is rooted in the self-activity of the working class.

This was even more the case when it came to the Gotha Program's statement, "The working class strives for its emancipation first of all *within the framework of the present-day national state*." This was not the first (or the last!) time that such nationalist verbiage found its way into the program of a "revolutionary" party—the founding program of the "Marxist" Eisenachers in 1869 contained similar language. But to assert this after years of work by the First International—which the ADAV refused to join, in contrast with the SDAP, which was a constituent member— seemed all the more inexplicable. The Gotha Program was slightly revised by Bebel and Liebknecht after Marx sent them (in private correspondence) his *Critique of the Gotha Program*, and the phrase the "present-day national state" was removed; but that hardly meant that the attitude that produced the error was stamped out. While it may be a stretch to suggest a direct line between the Gotha Program of 1875 and the "Great Betrayal" of 1914, when the SPD voted to approve of World War I, the seeds were clearly planted that far back.

Most important, as against the Gotha's Program's failure to deal with "the future body politic [*Staatswesen*] of communist society," Marx delves directly into a discussion of *what happens after a successful revolution* by distinguishing between a lower and higher phase of communism. The word "socialism" never appears in the *Critique*, since for Marx socialism and communism are completely interchangeable terms. *They are not distinct historical stages*. One of the biggest barriers to understanding the text is that post-Marx Marxists (most notably Lenin) falsely read into it a distinction between socialism and communism. This remains the lens through which most approach the *Critique* to this day. For example, Lucien Sève, a philosopher and former member of the French Communist Party, was shocked to discover belatedly that the distinction between socialism and communism that he (along with many others) was raised on is not found in Marx's writings.[13]

What defines the lower phase of socialism/communism, which is tainted by the "birthmarks" of the old world from which it emerges? In this initial, lower phase, Marx writes, the producers "do not exchange their products; just as little does the labor employed on the product appear here *as the value* of these products, as a material quality possessed by them, since now, in contrast to capitalist society, individual labor no longer exists in an indirect fashion but directly as a component part of the total labor."

Commodity exchange comes to an end in the initial phase of communism, since now that the producers freely control the means of production, abstract labor—the substance of value that enables products of labor to be universally exchanged—no longer exists. But how can products of labor be exchanged for one another if the social substance that is common to them no longer exists? The answer is that they cannot. An exchange of *activities* replaces the exchange of *products*. Retail trade, commerce and "the market" die away. Sharing, based on use values, replaces selling, based on exchange values. Directly social labor replaces indirectly social labor. With democratic, freely associated control of the means of production, the producers themselves, and not an external force such as socially necessary labor time, govern their interactions. Value production comes to an end *from the very inception* of a socialist or communist society.

Neither here nor anywhere else in discussing a postcapitalist society does Marx so much as mention the state. The state for Marx is abolished by the time we reach socialism or communism, since its basis, class society, is long gone.

Labor itself, however, is not abolished in the lower phase. Instead, *actual* labor time becomes a measure for distributing the products of communal activity. Marx writes, "Accordingly, the individual producer receives back from society, after the deductions have been made, exactly what he gives to it. What he has given to it is his individual *quantum* of labor." Individuals receive a voucher or token that they have "furnished such and such an amount of labor" to the community and from it obtain "the societal supply of means of consumption as much as the amount of labor cost." Marx is *not* suggesting that the workers' labor is computed on the basis of a social *average* of labor time that is imposed on them by an external force, such as the market or the state. Here, labor time simply refers to the actual number of hours of work performed by individuals.

This does not mean that workers cannot *take account* of the average amount of actual labor time it takes to create a given set of goods and services and arrange their working time in light of it. For example, workers in a number of different cooperatives may produce the same product in different amounts of time and choose to share information concerning the average amount in order to produce something faster (so they need not work as many hours) or slower (so as to increase the quality of the work or the product). But since they are in complete control of this time determination, the average does not assert itself as an independent law to which they are forced to submit. Social averages take on a totally different meaning in socialism as compared with capitalism.

Individuals are compensated by the community on the basis of the actual hours that they labor, without regard to their background, job, race, gender, skills, or "professional" status (those unable to work outside the home or who perform domestic labor such as childrearing are freely provided with goods and services). The existence of this formal measure ensures that neither individual officials nor political institutions decide how much anyone receives: such subjective factors (often subject to abuse) are foreclosed by labor time calculation.[14] Although Marx does not mention it, this seriously undermines the possibility of economic discrimination based on one's race, gender, or sexual orientation.[15]

He implies this in writing that individuals are "grasped only in terms of a specific aspect, for instance, in the present case, are regarded *only as workers* and nothing more is seen in them, everything else being ignored." He is not suggesting that people matter only insofar as they are workers or sources of economic output; on the contrary, when it comes to their *amount of compensation* everything is ignored except the actual hours of labor they perform. This allows us to live our lives as we choose without having to suffer from discriminatory economic policies based upon the personal prejudices of others.

Since no two individuals are exactly alike and they freely decide how much or little to work, some will receive more compensation than others. Social classes are abolished, but inequalities persist. The application of an equal standard (actual labor time) to unlike individuals leads to unequal levels of compensation. Marx never adhered to the crude notion that in "socialism" everyone earns exactly the same amount.

It has often been claimed that Marx is saying that in the lower phase the prevailing principle is "from each according to their ability, to each according to their *work*." This implies that one who produces more than another in the same unit of time earns greater compensation. But this is exactly what Marx is *not* saying. Each individual is compensated solely on the number of hours that she works, "everything else being ignored."[16] Through *this* principle all vestiges of wage labor are abolished.

The distinction between actual labor time and socially necessary labor time as a measure of the individual share of the social product is absolutely crucial, since conflating them leads to the erroneous view—shared by both market and statist socialists—that socially necessary labor time is an inevitable part of the human condition that will always be with us. But if that is so, it follows that the measure of socially average labor that imposes itself behind our backs, with all its alienated and dehumanizing characteristics, will always be with us. In that case, the "new" society becomes defined by the principles that govern the old one.

It may come as a surprise that Marx discusses the lower phase at greater length than a higher one, defined by "from each according to his abilities, to each according to his needs." Raya Dunayevskaya explained the reason: "To this day, this remains the perspective for the future, and yet the Marxists who keep quoting it never bother to study just how concretely that arose from the *Critique* of a supposedly socialist program, *and what would be required to make that real*."[17]

A postcapitalist society cannot immediately realize from each according to their abilities, to each according to their needs, since it is bound to emerge tainted with the "birthmarks" of the old society; the "muck of the ages" does not vanish overnight. This is especially the case because from each according to their abilities, to each according to their needs, involves the completely free and spontaneous allocation of goods and services—something that can only arise, Marx emphasizes, after a specific set of historical conditions are met. He specifies this as follows: "*After* the enslaving subordination of the individual to the division of labor, and thereby also the antithesis between mental and physical labor, has vanished;[18] *after* labor has become not only a means of life but life's prime desire and necessity [*erste Lebensbedürfniss*]; *after* the productive forces have also increased with the all-round development of the individual, and all the springs of cooperative wealth flow more abundantly, *only then* can ... society inscribe on its banners: From each according to his ability, to each according to his need!" For this reason, Marx begins his discussion of the new society with the initial, lower phase of socialism/communism that can make it possible for this cherished goal to become a reality. Creating a new society is therefore not a one-shot event but a *process*.

Labor time calculation as the form of organizing production and distribution that corresponds to the new relations of production is not some *ought* or subjective wish that Marx imposes upon the future. He is instead thinking out the social relations in the lower phase that would facilitate the subsequent development of the principle governing a higher phase. We must first learn how to control ourselves and our environment freed of such abstract forms of domination as socially necessary labor time and wealth expressed in monetary terms. Once this is achieved, along with the end of the opposition between mental and manual labor, the "all-round development of the individual," and "all springs of cooperative wealth [that] flow more abundantly," a higher phase can be reached in which labor becomes "life's prime desire and necessity"—that is, an end in itself instead of a mere means to an end. The lower phase will in due course give rise to a higher one that dispenses with actual labor time as a measure, since we will by then have learned to live without being governed by a quid pro quo—that is, I give X to you on condition that you give Y to me. At that point, *free time*, not labor time, will serve as the measure of human development. The assumption that social relations based on a quid pro quo are "natural" and will forever define our person-to-person interactions has been bred into us by thousands of years of class society, but it will be looked upon as an odd anachronism by the time we reach a socialist/communist society "based on its own foundations."[19]

The lower phase is still *defective*, since (as Marx notes) there is a "parallel" with commodity production *in the very restricted sense* that it is governed by an exchange of equivalents. As with "bourgeois right," what one gets from society depends on what one gives to it. But this quid pro quo is a world removed from the exchange of *abstract* equivalents. *What gets exchanged are human activities, not products bearing a value-form.* This means that on at least one level contractual relations continue to exist in the lower phase. But since these are *freely* associated and not mediated by hierarchical class relations or abstract forms of domination, they could not be more different from the contractual forms that prevail in capitalism, wherein the seemingly "free" exchange of labor power for wages belies a fundamentally unfree system of exploitation.

Since Marx's discussion of "bourgeois right" as prevailing in the lower phase is easily misconstrued, it is worth pausing to examine the issue more closely. As noted earlier, a *measure* is needed to determine how much compensation the individual obtains from the communal storehouse. This will not be an issue once from each according to their abilities, to each according to their needs prevails. But what happens in a new society that emerges from the womb of the old one in which this principle does not yet prevail? Simply asserting that it will now be based on use values instead of exchange values does not suffice, for it leaves undetermined how to apportion the various use values to members of the community. A measure or yardstick is needed to determine the proper proportion between producers' contribution to society and what they receive from it—otherwise, production and consumption will be out of sync and society will quickly unravel. Marx's response is that given the specific conditions facing a society "as it emerges" from the old one, "bourgeois right" prevails insofar as what you get depends on what you give. This does not mean that the bourgeoisie or classes persist; it means that the *form* of an equal exchange exists—albeit one possessing an altogether different content than under capitalism. In capitalism, the legal fiction ("bourgeois right") is that you receive from society a material equivalent of your labor contribution. Of course, this claim of an "equal exchange" between labor power and capital, which is central to wage labor, is completely fallacious, since workers contribute far more than their level of compensation. But the *form* of a quid pro quo carries over into the lower phase of socialism/communism (only now without any false conflation of appearance and reality) insofar as workers are compensated based on the amount of actual labor time performed.

But since this measure is not an abstract average imposed upon us against our will but an expression of what we freely decide to do with our time, it is more than likely that we will choose to work as few hours as possible in order to enjoy the many fruits of life outside of labor—such as caring for each other, engaging in cultural and artistic pursuits, enjoying nature, etc. As Marx notes elsewhere, the economization of labor time is a principle that governs all forms of society. Now that social relations are freely associated, an incentive is finally provided for investing in technologies that free people from work instead of chaining them to it.[20] At the same time, since indirectly social relations based on exchange value, money, and abstract labor are eliminated in the lower phase of socialism/communism, people learn to treat each other as ends in themselves instead of as mere means to an end. The ground is now laid for moving beyond "bourgeois right" and labor time as a measure toward a higher phase defined by from each according to their abilities, to each according to their needs.

One might ask: but why all this fuss about distinguishing a lower from a higher phase of a new society? Why not just call the former "socialism" and the latter "communism," as so many did in the twentieth century? In actuality, there are extremely serious *political* consequences to presuming that "socialism" and "communism" are distinct forms of society—so serious as to warrant careful consideration.

For any historical materialist, societies are defined by distinct modes of production. Slave societies had a particular mode of production that was different from feudalism; feudalism had a particular mode of production that was different from capitalism; and capitalism has a particular mode of production that is different from socialism. If "socialism" and "communism" are distinct forms of society, they must be characterized by different modes of production. But what could that difference be?

As noted above, for Marx the capitalist mode of production is defined by the drive to augment value, or wealth in monetary form, as an end in itself. This is because the capitalist mode of production is based on abstract or alienated labor. In contrast, socialism is a completely distinct mode of production, since it is defined by the free association of producers, who (as Marx put it in Volume III of *Capital*) "bring the productive process under their common control by their associated reason."[21] This means that abstract or alienated labor is abolished in socialism, as are classes and other forms of domination (such as socially necessary labor time as a measure of the individual share in the social product). But if "communism" is a different social formation from socialism, it must have a distinctive mode of production. But what could this be? Is it possible that in "communism" there is no longer a free association of producers who "bring the productive process under their common control by their associated reason"? That clearly makes no sense. This is why Marx uses "socialism" and "communism" as synonyms throughout his work.

But if one still insists on viewing socialism and communism as distinct forms of society, the logical conclusion is to divest "socialism" of its liberatory content by posing "communism" as the realm freed from value production, and "socialism" as the statist management of value production through nationalized property and a planned economy. How else could one define the alleged difference in their modes of production? And this is exactly how it was defined by most twentieth-century Marxists. The emancipatory promise of a new society—the abolition of alienated labor, the end of producing for the sake of augmenting monetary wealth, and the free association of the producers—was pushed off to the far distant "communist" horizon, while the masses were told to suffer the indignities of statist repression, forced labor, and statist management of value production in the name of "socialism."[22] As a result, the very *concept* of socialism, which had excited the imagination of hundreds of millions worldwide, became besmirched to the point that today many identify it not with freedom but dictatorship and even genocide.

In a word, posing "socialism" and "communism" as distinct historical social formations pushes the idea of freedom off to a far-distant future that never comes, while divesting the idea of socialism of its liberatory content. Such is the price that is paid for considering crucial theoretical determinations as mere academic hair-splitting.

IV

It is safe to say that none of the leading tendencies that sought to chart a path beyond capitalism since Marx's time based themselves on the principles outlined in the *Critique of the Gotha Program*. Why this is so requires several levels of explanation.

Marx did not publish the *Critique of the Gotha Program*, so its existence was known by only a handful of people at the time. He abstained from doing so mainly because several leaders of the new party that drafted the Program were facing persecution and jail by the German government. It was first published after Marx's death by Engels in 1891, on the eve of the drafting of a new program for the SAPD, now renamed the SPD. Although Engels was critical of the SPD's Erfurt Program (mainly authored by Karl Kautsky), absent from it were such openly Lassallean phrases as "labor is the source of all wealth," the "iron law of wages," and calls for the capitalist state to fund worker cooperatives. It therefore appeared to many who took the trouble to read the *Critique of the Gotha Program* at the time that it had been overtaken by the more recent (and slightly improved) Erfurt Program, which soon became the basis for virtually all socialist parties in Europe and beyond.

This does not fully explain, however, why even Marx's closest German followers paid little or no attention to the *Critique*, both before and after its publication. A critical factor was the assumption that while Marx was a great theoretician, Lassalle was the one to follow when it came to organization. It was Lassalle, after all, who founded the first independent workers' party in Germany, in 1863—at a time when Marx was buried in the British Museum writing *Capital* and less involved in organizational affairs. And it was Lassalle who authored a series of best-selling pamphlets that popularized the socialist message in a language that was relatively easy to understand—in contrast to Marx's complex and difficult theoretical works. It is hard today to appreciate the immense popularity of Lassalle in the last several decades of the nineteenth and early twentieth century—he was a revered figure even by those who disagreed with much of his politics. His popularity was not limited to Europe; one of the first US translations of parts of Volume I of *Capital* appeared in the journal *The Socialist* (in thirteen installments, beginning in May 1876), a publication founded in 1874 by followers of Lassalle.

Moreover, because the SDAP rapidly grew in size after uniting with the Lassalleans—and the SPD (by 1891 part of the Second International) that succeeded it became even larger, exceeding a million members—it seemed to many that Marx's *Critique* had lost its relevance. Why worry about Marx's objection to some theoretical differences with Lassalle in the far distant past when the party was now so successful?

It should not be presumed that Lassalle's influence was restricted to reformist socialists (who surely deeply admired him); he was no less influential among revolutionary socialists such as Lenin and Rosa Luxemburg, who were Lassalleans when it came to organizational matters. The much-vaunted concept of "vanguard party to lead" was *not* the invention of Lenin; it was the invention of *Lassalle*, who bequeathed it to German Social Democracy—which in turn gifted it to Russian Marxism.

This separation of organizational practice from theory among Marx's closest followers was perhaps most revealingly expressed by Liebknecht, who said of Marx's *Critique*, "Theory and practice are two different things. As unconditionally as I trust Marx's judgment in theory, so in practice I go my own way."[23]

There was another reason for the pervasive silence over Marx's *Critique*: the widespread prohibition against saying anything substantial about a future society. Though this was justified on "materialist" grounds (often with quotes lifted from Marx), it took on the form of a religious incantation. As one recent study put it, "The successors of Marx and Engels imposed a strict ban on dealing with the fundamental principles of a communist economic and social order. Failure to comply would lead to accusations of engaging in 'fake science.' One was allowed to praise communism, but not allowed to think about it."[24] The new society was treated along the lines of Kant's unknowable thing-in-itself ("we know it's there but we dare not speak of it"). Given such attitudes, Marx's discussion of the lower and higher phases of a new society in the *Critique* seemed an odd anomaly. Such attitudes prevail even today, as seen in those who praise socialism as superior to capitalism but convince themselves not to think about it when pressed as to what that *means*. They therefore spend much of their lives pursuing an empty signifier.

Matters began to change only in 1917, when the February Revolution that brought down the Russian Empire raised the prospect of imminent socialist revolutions. As Lenin prepared for a "second chapter" of the revolution in the ensuing months, he turned to Marx's *Critique of the Gotha Program*—issuing the most extensive discussion of it by anyone since Marx's death in his book *The State and Revolution*. Lenin profoundly discussed aspects of Marx's *Critique* that were completely overlooked by the Marxists of the Second International—especially its insistence that the task is not to "take over" the existing state but to *smash* it. Nevertheless, there were two major problems with Lenin's effort to appropriate the *Critique of the Gotha Program* for the realities of his time. First, despite his acceptance of Marx's critique of his followers for adhering to the doctrines of Lassalle, Lenin did not draw from it the need to break from the elitist concept of the vanguard party to lead, which derived from Lassalle. In fact, there is virtually no discussion of "the party" in *The State and Revolution* at all. Lenin did not see Marx's *Critique* as pointing to a different concept of organization from what prevailed in the Second (and later the Third) International.[25] Second, Lenin misconstrued aspects of Marx's treatment of the lower phase of socialism/communism by ignoring his discussion of labor time calculation and arguing instead that wage labor prevails in socialism (which he wrongly identifies as a distinct social formation from communism) insofar as all citizens become hired employees of the state.[26] This is highly problematic, since the Marxist understanding is that wage labor cannot exist without capital and capital cannot exist without wage labor. Lenin was therefore suggesting that "socialism" represents the state-management and allocation of capital rather than its *abolition* through the formation of new human relations in which the products of labor no longer dominate the producers.

Lenin was at least honest enough to openly admit shortly after the Bolshevik Revolution in October 1917 that he and his colleagues had not a clue as to how to affect a transition to socialism. Such was the impact of the decades-long prohibition against saying anything about a future society! In Russia's case, there was of course the added issue that virtually no Marxist prior to Lenin's "April Theses" of 1917 thought that a transition to socialism was currently on the agenda in Russia. For decades both wings of Russian Marxism had argued that Russia's "backwardness" meant that the most that could be immediately achieved is a bourgeois-democratic regime that creates the economic preconditions for a subsequent socialist revolution. (The difference between the Bolsheviks and Mensheviks centered on which class was to lead the bourgeois-democratic revolution.)

Expectations that the spread of the Bolshevik Revolution to other lands would inaugurate the transition to socialism nevertheless ran high in the years immediately following 1917;

this was the "magic" of the Russian Revolution that excited the imagination of millions of people from Germany to China, from India to Scotland, from South Africa to the USA. At first, the Bolsheviks adopted "war communism"—based on shutting down free markets, moving away from money by paying workers in kind rather than cash, and expropriating grain from the peasants. Though the Bolsheviks were trying to get away from using money as the measure that determines the proportion between production and consumption, they did not present any alternative form of economic measure; everything was determined by the whim of government officials. By 1921, when the hoped-for revolutions in Western Europe failed to materialize, Lenin admitted that such economic policies were leading the country to collapse and shifted gears by introducing the New Economic Policy (NEP)—a "step back to capitalism" defined by a mixed economy of free markets and the state controlling the "commanding heights" of heavy industry. Lenin, to his credit, never claimed that "war communism" or the NEP constituted "socialism"; he, like virtually all Marxists before Stalin, held that it is impossible for socialism to exist in one country. It takes an *international* revolution.

That vision died with Stalin's rise to power, the forced industrialization drive of the 1930s, and his declaration in 1936 that "socialism" was now "irrevocably established" with the complete nationalization of property. Yet it began to become clear to some dissident Marxists (the anarchists saw this much earlier) that what had actually come into being was a new version of capitalism, *state-capitalism*. By 1944, even Stalin had to address why so many elements associated with capitalism—prices, average rates of profit, cost accounting, social hierarchy, and statist repression—could exist under "socialism." It led to his sudden declaration in the midst of World War II that the law of value—which had been previously considered the hallmark of capitalism—operated in the USSR and in any other future "socialist" society, albeit "in the interests of the masses." This stunning revision in the Marxian concept of the law of value, which was translated and published with a critical commentary by Dunayevskaya in *The*

American Economic Review in 1944, established the template for all the "communist" regimes that followed.[27]

With the rise of Stalinism and the spread of "Marxist-Leninist" ideology in the decades that followed, the perspective contained in the *Critique of the Gotha Program* receded ever further from view. There were exceptions: Jan Appel, a German revolutionary influenced by the council communism of Anton Pannekoek, published in his 1930 *Fundamental Principles of Communist Production and Distribution*, which used Marx's *Critique* to delineate the economic basis of communism. It received very little attention at the time. (It has recently been issued in a new English translation.)[28] But such efforts to return to Marx's *Critique* were few and far between.

There are two closely related *conceptual* reasons that most Marxists have not taken up the insights found in the *Critique of the Gotha Program*. One concerns how the socialization of the means of production is widely understood; the other is the assumption that capitalism is defined by "market anarchy" and socialism by "central planning."

Most socialists and communists have presumed—and many still do—that collectivized property is the *aim* of a new society. This was never Marx's or Engels's view: they held that it is a necessary but insufficient step toward its creation. The abolition of private property does not involve simply getting rid of the property right of individual capitalists; it involves getting rid of *any* entity or grouping, under whatever name, which instead of the producers controls the means of production. Collective ownership of the means of production *by the freely associated producers* enables them to eliminate forced and alienated labor. But it is not an end in itself. It is one *step* in a prolonged process of transforming alienated human relations—in the workplace, between men and women, among different races and ethnicities, and in how we treat the natural environment. As Dunayevskaya put it in her first essay analyzing the Soviet Union as a state-capitalist society in 1941, "The determining factor in analyzing the class nature of a society is not whether the means of production are the private property of the capitalist class or are state-owned, but whether the means of production are *capital*, that is, whether they are monopolized and alienated from the direct producers."[29]

Closely connected with the above, post-Marx Marxists almost universally viewed the fundamental distinction between capitalism and socialism as "the anarchy of the market" versus "planned production." This assumption ran very deep—to the extent that it was taken for granted by reformists and revolutionaries, authoritarians and antiauthoritarians. As far back as 1891, Engels took issue with this in his critique of the Erfurt Program (written mainly by Kautsky, who later became known as "the Pope of Marxism"). Engels wrote, "What is capitalist *private* production? Production by separate entrepreneurs, which is increasingly becoming an exception. Capitalist production by *joint-stock companies* is no longer *private* production but production on behalf of many associated people. And when we pass on from joint-stock companies to trusts, which dominate and monopolize whole branches of industry, this puts an end not only to private production but also to *planlessness*."[30]

Unfortunately, this criticism was not heard by Engels's associates, who continued to define capitalism as "unplanned" and socialism as "planned." The result is that "socialism" became defined as a more equitable or efficient way of organizing exchange. Left totally out of the picture is that exchange relations in capitalism are already "organized"—albeit in a totally irrational way—by the law of value, which compels human activity to correspond to the dictates of socially necessary labor time. By focusing on the superficial, phenomenal level of exchange relations instead of the underlying time determination that governs *production* relations, post-Marx Marxists lost sight of the depth of the uprooting needed to put an end to capitalism. No wonder that they paid little attention to Marx's discussion of the difference between socially necessarily labor time and actual labor time in the *Critique of the Gotha Program*.

V

In more recent decades, with the collapse of the Stalinist regimes and Marxist-Leninist ideology, on the one hand, and the emergence of a new generation of anticapitalist, antiracist, antisexist theorists and activists on the other, Marx's *Critique of the Gotha Program* has become subject to increased discussion and debate. Generally, these discussions tend to fall into two camps: one argues that the principles outlined by Marx are utopian and unrealistic, the other that the *Critique* offers a model of exactly how a postcapitalist society ought to be constructed. Marxist-Humanists differ from both positions. Marx's concept of the two phases of communism is remarkably visionary, but also strikingly realistic. He does not presume that "from each according to his ability, to each according to his needs" can be achieved by a mere act of will. It depends on a series of specific social and historical conditions. For the same reason, Marx is not presenting a set of recipes about exactly how to organize a postcapitalist society. He is presenting guiding concepts that he sees as being overlooked in the workers' movement.

At the same time, it is a mistake to read Marx's *Critique* too literally by assuming that social relations in the lower phase are completely defined by remuneration based on actual labor time. First, the amount of time employed in laboring would be much less than under capitalism, since the abolition of value production removes the social incentive to grow the economy as an end in itself. Marx repeatedly argues throughout his writings that the reduction of labor time in favor of free time is a fundamental prerequisite of a postcapitalist society. Second, Marx explicitly insists in the *Critique* that the labor involved in raising children, education, health care, and social welfare would be compensated on the basis of need through a common fund. They are not subject to the exchange of actual labor time for goods and services. This is, again, why he takes sharp issue with the Gotha Program's call for producers to receive the "undiminished" product of their labor: if laborers receive as much wealth as they produce it would be impossible to meet the needs of entire sections of society. Hence, certain types of labor and human activity are not subject to any quid pro quo, even in the lower phase of communism. Third, even today some people (though not enough!) enjoy their work and perform it with little or no expectation of return; this is especially evident among those working in open source, software, and peer production who provide goods and services without the slightest material incentive. This would surely be far more widespread in a post-capitalist society, which would provide the space for individuals to discover themselves and freely pursue their destinies, now that such external impediments as class domination, statist control, and abstract forms of domination no longer stand in their way. Fourth, by no longer being subject to an abstract time determination outside of their control, individuals will have the freedom to decide how much or little of their time to devote to work and material acquisitions, thereby impelling the move toward a higher phase of socialism/communism in which labor time is no longer a social determinant. Hence, as the Group of International Communists writes, "although working time plays the role of being the measure for individual distribution, this measure will be destroyed in the course of its development."[31]

One discussion by antistatist Marxists in *Endnotes* typifies the difficulties many encounter with Marx's text. This discussion takes Marx's treatment of distribution according to actual labor time to mean that the lower phase of communism represents universalized value production: "The universalization of this form of domination is the precursor to the end of domination. For Marx, it is only in the higher phase that domination is actually overcome."[32] It is hard to see how this can be read into Marx's text, since in the lower phase there are no classes, no alienated or abstract labor, no commodity exchange, and no dual character of labor. *Endnotes* appears to base its argument on the earlier English translation, which renders Marx, in speaking of the lower phase of communism, as stating, "Here, obviously, the same principle prevails as that which regulates the exchange of commodities, as far as this is exchange involving equal values." Since the author interprets "equal values" to mean equal *exchange values*, they conclude that Marx's view is that the central principle of social domination in capitalism, the law of value, operates in "socialism."[33] This is a very common misinterpretation.

A more recent discussion by the Chinese scholar Tian Yu Cao states of the same passage, "Essentially, what Marx said here is that law of value will still be operative in a socialist society, although there are restrictions: nothing but labor can enter into exchange, and nothing can pass to the ownership of the means of production."[34] However, the phrase "exchange involving equal values" is a mistranslation; the correct translation is "exchange involving equal *worth*." The German word "Wert" can be translated as either "value" or "worth," depending on the context. There is a vast difference between the two in English: *value* refers to wealth in monetary form which takes the form of exchange value on the market, while *worth* often refers to material wealth or use values. Marx is surely referring to the latter, *an exchange of equal use values* (one hour of actual labor time is exchanged for goods produced in one hour), since just a few paragraphs earlier he writes, "the producers do not exchange their products; just as little does the labor expended on the products appear here *as the value* of these products." Either Marx is an extremely sloppy and inconsistent thinker or the above commentators get it wrong. They indeed get it wrong, for they are (no doubt unconsciously) reading into the text an interpretation that dovetails with Stalin's 1944 declaration that the law of value operates in "socialism"—a conception that very few Marxists had earlier entertained. Both writers cited above are principled *anti*-Stalinists; but that does not stop the ideological pollution propagated for decades by so-called "Marxist-Leninists" to penetrate the way even independent Marxists sometimes read Marx's texts.

What may also explain the above (mis)interpretations is a notion that has greater support in some of Marx's writings—namely, that free time and not labor time would be the measure in a postcapitalist society. This is most explicitly expressed in a section of Marx's *Grundrisse*, which traces out the ultimate outcome of capitalism's drive to increase labor productivity by replacing workers with machines and automated devices:

> Labor no longer appears so much as included in the production process, but rather man relates himself to

that process as its overseer and regulator.... Once this transformation has taken place, it is neither the immediate labor performed by man himself, nor the time for which he works, but the appropriation of his own general productive power, his comprehension of Nature and domination of it by virtue of his being a social entity—in a word, the development of the social individual—that appears as the cornerstone of production and wealth.... As soon as labor time in its immediate form ceases to be the great source of wealth, labor time ceases and must cease to be its measure, and therefore exchange value [must cease to be the measure] of use value.[35]

By "labor time" Marx here refers to socially necessary labor time, not the actual labor time that serves as the measure in a lower phase of socialism/communism. His point is that by displacing labor from the process of production through technological innovations, the very basis of value production eventually becomes undermined. Labor becomes essentially "abolished." At that point, the basis is provided for a new society that is no longer tied to abstract universal labor time as the measure of social relations.

Numerous thinkers have taken this to mean that transcending capitalism and creating socialism depends upon the *abolition* of labor rather than the emancipation of labor.[36] This has become a favored position by many radical intellectuals in recent years, especially in light of the decline of the organized labor movement and with it the end of their hopes for a "proletarian" revolution.[37] Obviously, if "labor" comes to an end in socialism, not just abstract universal labor time, but also actual labor time cannot serve as a measure in the lower phase of socialism/communism. By this reasoning, any effort to posit actual labor time as a measure presupposes the continued existence of value production. Yet Marx clearly argues in the *Critique of the Gotha Program* that distribution according to actual labor time represents the annulment of value production. There *appears* to be a contradiction between these two different texts by Marx. The way that most advocates of the "abolition of labor" respond to this apparent contradiction is by simply ignoring the discussion in the *Critique of the Gotha Program*.

There is no question that for Marx the reduction of labor time to a minimum is a fundamental precondition of socialism/communism. "Labor" is made into a false absolute in capitalism since labor is the source of value, and all capitalism cares about is augmenting value as an end in itself. A postcapitalist society that overcomes value production would therefore privilege free time over labor time. Yet in Volume I of *Capital*—published a decade after the *Grundrisse* and his most mature and developed reflection on these issues—Marx *denies* that labor will be abolished in socialism/communism.[38] He writes:

> Only the abolition of the capitalist form of production would permit the reduction of the working day to the necessary labor time. But even in that case the latter would expand to take up more of the day, and for two reasons: first, because the worker's conditions of life would improve, and his aspirations become greater, and second, because a part of what is now surplus labor would then count as necessary labor, namely, the labor which is necessary for the formation of a social fund for reserve and accumulation.[39]

By the time he wrote *Capital*, Marx makes explicit that it is not labor per se that is abolished in a new society but rather industrial, "productive" labor that augments surplus value. However, not all labor is constitutive of value production. He writes in *Capital*, "Labor is the universal condition for the metabolic interaction between the human being and nature, the everlasting nature-imposed condition of human existence, and it is therefore ... common to all forms of society in which humans live."[40] The *Critique of the Gotha Program* is completely consistent with this in stating that even "in a higher phase of communist society ... labor has become not only a means of life but life's prime desire and necessity."

Even if we put aside the question of whether an interpretation is faithful to Marx's texts (after all, his ideas are not gospel and always call for critical examination), the claim that his discussion of remuneration according to actual labor time is compatible with value production makes sense only if "labor" of any kind is equated with abstract labor, and "time" of any kind is equated with abstract universal labor time. Such claims may be consistent with the logic of capital, but they hardly do much to enable us to envision an alternative to it.

The *Critique of the Gotha Program* helps show how, at least for Marx, socialism, even in its most initial phase, represents a far sharper break from capitalism and a far more liberatory form of society than has generally been appreciated for the last hundred years.[41] To go from capitalism to socialism/communism is to go from a world in which individuals are dominated by their own creations to one that is freely associated; from one defined by the accumulation of money and profit to one defined by the expression of our creative powers; from one in which we are treated as means to an end to one in which we are treated as ends-in-themselves. But this raises a big question: How do we get from here to there? Surely, socialism/communism does not just instantly arise upon making a revolution. What form of transition is needed to get there?

Marx addresses this, albeit briefly, in the *Critique*, in discussing "the dictatorship of the proletariat." This should not be confused with the initial phase of socialism or communism. The *Critique* clearly defines the *"revolutionary* dictatorship of the proletariat" as a *political* transitional period *between* capitalism and the new society. He writes, "Between capitalist and communist society lies the period . . . in which the state can be nothing but *the revolutionary dictatorship of the proletariat.*" The term "dictatorship" is somewhat misleading, since Marx did not mean a dictatorship of a party or group lording it over the masses. At the time he wrote the *Critique*, the term referred to the mass of the oppressed *dictating* their will against the old ruling classes. It signifies democratic control of society by the "immense majority," the oppressed, who use political power as a *lever* to crush any impending counterrevolution, eliminate the political power and property rights of the capitalists, and move on by revolutionizing the social relations of production and reproduction. This has nothing to do with centralizing state power in the hands of the working class upon seizing power. On the contrary, as he specifies in his writings on the Paris Commune, the dictatorship of the proletariat represents the *suppression* of state power by the organized power of *society*. He restates this in the *Critique*: "Freedom consists in converting the state from an organ super-imposed upon society into one completely subordinate to it." He conceives of this as a transitional *period* (not to be confused with a transitional *society*) in which *masses* of people—workers, women, youth, and national minorities—use multiple forms of association and organization to wrest control of society from the exploiters. Because of this transition period's thoroughly *democratic* form, and the misleading nature of the word "dicta-torship," it may be best today to come up with a different term. In any case, Marx holds that once socialism or communism is reached, the dictatorship of the proletariat becomes superfluous, since with the end of class society the proletariat is abolished alongside all other classes. *And at that point the state as such comes to an end as well.*

By confusing the "dictatorship of the proletariat" with the initial phase of socialism or communism, many have assumed that the state—which in a limited form prevails in the political transition period—also continues in socialism/communism. Often misread is Marx's question in the *Critique*, "What transfor-mation will the form of the state undergo in communist society?" This is a mistranslation. The original does not speak of the "form of the state" in communism; it speaks of former state functions (*Staatswesen*—not *Staat*) that can readily be employed without a state. This is made clear by the next sentence: "In other words, what social functions analogous to present state functions will remain at that juncture?" Marx makes it clear throughout his writings that socialism or communism is incompatible with the state, since the latter is an "excrescence" of class society that is superseded in a postcapitalist society.[42]

This point is often missed. As Michael Lebowitz wrote a few years ago in *The Socialist Alternative: From Gotha to Now*, "We build communist society *upon its own foundations* by developing new communal relations of production that subordinate the private ownership of labor power *by creating a new state.*"[43] In direct contrast to Marx, Lebowitz imports the state not only into the lower phase of communism but also a higher phase as well, since Marx defines the latter as "a communist society on its own foundations"! How does he manage that in an otherwise detailed analysis of the *Critique*? He does so by claiming that the lower phase is characterized by the contradiction between socialized means of production and the "private ownership of labor power." In the initial phase of socialism, he contends, individuals "sell" their labor power to the collective, which means, he writes, that the alienation of the product from the producer and the alienation of person from person still exists in "socialism." A strong, centralized state is therefore needed to manage the inevitable conflicts that arise. He hangs his entire argument on the presumed existence of "the private ownership of labor power," even though such a term or concept never appears in Marx's text. Nor could it, since as Marx writes in *Capital* in describing the new society, "free human beings ... expend their many different forms of labor power in full self-awareness as *one single force.*"[44] This means, as Hermann Lueer writes, that "no longer is the individual labor of each member of society a private asset to be sold on the market for goods and labor for it to be recognized as having social value."[45] Lebowitz imports concepts that have nothing to do with what Marx says in the *Critique* in order to justify his approach of fetishizing the state as an eternal fact of human existence.

But the question remains, *why* does he do so? Lebowitz was an advisor to Hugo Chávez's government in Venezuela, which despite its accomplishments in redistributing oil revenue to the masses through social welfare programs, built up a highly centralized state while refraining from abolishing the private ownership of labor power (a shortcoming that later came to haunt the regime, especially under Maduro). He therefore seeks to justify Chávez's approach by reading it back into Marx. It is one thing to seek to explain the gains (and some of the shortcomings) of the "Bolivarian Revolution." It is quite another to do so at the cost of truncating the expansive vision of freedom found in Marx's *Critique of the Gotha Program*.

It is vital for us in the twenty-first century, faced with the urgent task of developing a *viable* concept of an *emancipatory* alternative to capitalism, to avoid the dead ends and halfway houses that have afflicted Marxists and other revolutionaries over the past 150 years. Marx does not give us the "answer" as to how to build a new society, but his work points us in an important direction. The destruction being wrought on society and nature by the relentless accumulation of value for its own sake is jeopardizing the future of life on this planet, but we still have time to make a new beginning in developing *revolutionary* perspectives for the *actual* transcendence of capitalism. We issue this book in the hope that it can help move this forward.

Notes

1 This essay is not an effort to summarize or analyze all aspects of Marx's *Critique of the Gotha Program*; it focuses exclusively on its discussion of the alternative to capitalism because of its direct relevance to the realities of our time.

2 See Marx's letter to F.A. Sorge, October 19, 1877, in *Marx-Engels Collected Works* (New York: International Publishers, 1988), 45:283: "In Germany a corrupt spirit is asserting itself in our party, not so much among the masses as the leaders (higher class and workers). The compromise with the Lassalleans has led to further compromise with other waverers."

3 Since the First International was composed of multiple tendencies French Proudhonists who opposed trade unions as well as English reformists who supported trade unions, communists, and anarchists, among others—Marx (as a leading figure in its Central Council) was obligated to maintain cordial relations with workers' associations or parties regardless of his estimate of them. This is probably why prior to 1874 he did not publicly object to aspects of the SDAP (especially its fondness for aspects of Lassalleanism) that is expressed in his private correspondence. By 1875, on the other hand, the First International was no longer in existence.

4 For a demonstration of this, see Peter Hudis, *Marx's Concept of the Alternative to Capitalism* (Chicago: Haymarket Books, 2013).

5 As Marx writes in chapter one of *Capital*, vol. I, translated by Ben Fowkes (New York: Penguin Books, 1977), 137, "In the physiological sense [human labor power] is this quality of being equal, or abstract human labor." This does not mean, however, that abstract labor is a transhistorical

phenomenon. It is the physiological expenditure of labor only in specific historical conditions.

6　*Capital* I:169.

7　*Capital* I:170. The Fowkes translation conveys "labor" in this sentence in the singular, whereas the German original has "labors." This is an important distinction, since "labors" makes it clear that Marx is talking of use values, whereas "labor" can be read as homogeneous labor that is the substance of exchange value. Marx consistently holds that the latter is annulled in a socialist or communist society. See *Marx-Engels Werke* (Berlin: Dietz Verlag, 1975), 23:91: "Aber eben weil persöhnliche Abhängigkeitsverhältnisse die gegebne gesellschäftliche Grundlage bilden, brauchen *Arbeiten* und Produkten nicht eine von ihrer Realität verschiedene phantastische Gestalt anzunehemen." I wish to thank Karel Ludenhoff for bringing this to my attention.

8　*Capital* I:171, trans. slightly altered.

9　*Capital* I:171–72.

10　Ibid., 165.

11　Jairus Banaji, "From the Commodity to Capital: Hegel's Dialectic in Marx's *Capital*," in *Value: The Representation of Labor in Capitalism*, ed. Diane Elson (London: Verso, 2015), 34.

12　For brilliant critique of "the iron law of wages," see Rosa Luxemburg's *Introduction to Political Economy*, in *Complete Works, Vol. I: Economic Writings 1*, ed. Peter Hudis (London: Verso, 2013), 288: "The trade union thus plays an indispensable organic role in the modern wage system. It is only through the union that labor-power as a commodity is placed in a position where it can be sold at its value. The capitalist law of value, in relation to labor-power, is not abolished by the trade unions, as [Ferdinand] Lassalle misguidedly assumed; on the contrary, it is only by their action that it is realized. The systematic giveaway price at which the capitalist seeks to buy labor-power is increasingly replaced by a more or less real price thanks to union action."

13　Lucien Sève, *Penser avec Marx aujourd'hui: I. Marx et nous* (Paris: La Dispute, 2004), 37. There is a world of difference between using "socialism" and "communism" to mean distinct *historical stages* and using them to define particular *political parties*. As Engels put it in his preface to the 1890 edition of *The Communist Manifesto* (originally published in 1847), "Socialism in 1847 signified a bourgeois movement, communism a working-class movement. Socialism was, on the continent at least, quite respectable, whereas communism was the very opposite. And since we were very decidedly of the opinion as early as then that 'the emancipation of the workers must be the task of the working class itself,' we could have no hesitation as to which of the two names we should choose" (*Marx-Engels Collected Works*, 17:60). In the 1860s, on the other hand, "socialism" no longer referred to a bourgeois reform movement but was adopted by *revolutionary* opponents of capitalism, including the followers of Marx.

14　The introduction of a uniform standard of measure across the whole of society likewise renders unnecessary the seemingly endless series of meetings and deliberations that characterize such models of a future society as Michael Albert's *Parecon: Life after Capitalism* (London: Verso, 2003).

15 The undermining of *economic* discrimination does not of course imply the end to all forms of discrimination; no formal economic measure, including labor time calculation, can on its own eliminate racism, sexism, and homophobia. These can only be overcome by the praxis of multiple subjects of revolt who contest discriminatory ideas and practices not only before but *after* the revolutionary seizure of power. This is clearly not possible where a single party or centralized state assumes control following a revolution. A truly new *human* society is a product of a *permanent* revolution.

16 A common objection to this approach is that it will allow slackers to work more slowly than others in order to obtain a greater quantity of goods. Such objections overlook the fact that in the lower phase the producers have effective and not just nominal control of the means of production. Since there can be only a finite number of goods in the common storehouse, an enterprise or cooperative can freely decide, through democratic deliberation, that such slackers receive less remuneration if engaging in such noncooperative activity. Needless to say, in no socialist revolution to date have the producers exercised effective and not just nominal control of the means of production.

17 Raya Dunayevskaya, *Rosa Luxemburg, Women's Liberation, and Marx's Philosophy of Revolution* (Atlantic Highlands, NJ: Humanities Press, 1981), 156–57. My emphasis.

18 Marx envisions an end to the "antithesis" or *antagonism* between mental and manual labor, not the elimination of one or the other. The *unity* of mental and manual labor, of thinking and doing, signifies a new kind of labor caught up with life—namely, *nonalienated* labor.

19 Even the most alienated form of society cannot suppress the intuition that our most valuable relations are not based on a quid pro quo. In loving someone we give to the other without expectation of return. The ancients viewed this as the most important source of happiness. Though less openly articulated in modern commercial societies, is it any less true today?

20 Although the claim has been made for decades that increased investment in machinery, automation, robotics, and now "artificial intelligence" will "free" us from unnecessary labor, this has never happened and will never happen so long as we have capitalism. The length of the working day throughout the world has only increased in recent decades. This would come as no surprise to Marx, who wrote, "machinery, considered alone, shortens the hours of labor, but when in the service of capital, lengthens them." See *Capital*, I:568.

21 Quoted in Seongjin Jeong, "Engels' Concept of Alternatives to Capitalism," paper presented to Conference on "Friedrich Engels—Die Aktualität eines Klassikers," February 2020, Wuppertal, Germany. This comment from Marx's original manuscript for vol. III of *Capital* was left out of the

published version edited by Engels as well as the 2016 translation of the manuscript by Ben Fowkes. For the latter, see *Marx's Economic Manuscript of 1864–1865*, ed. Fred Moseley (Leiden: Brill, 2016).

22 Once "socialism" was emptied of its liberatory content by being equated with value production, statist domination, and the complete suppression of democracy, it was only a matter of time before the same happened to the concept of "communism." Stalin's last work, *Economic Problems of Socialism* (1952), presents "full communism" as a military boot camp combining agricultural and productive labor. This directly influenced Mao Zedong's concept of total collectivization via "people's communes," which Pol Pot tried to put into practice in Cambodia. The results are well known.

23 This does not mean that Liebknecht and other Eisenachers excelled in their grasp of theory; Marx often complained that the Lassalleans took theory more seriously than his own followers. As Jenny Marx (his wife and intellectual collaborator) put it in a letter to Engels shortly after the founding of the SDAP, its "only effect seems to be to have helped 'our great master Ferdinand' [Lassalle] to obtain, in addition to his official '*moniteur*,' the *Social-Demokrat*, a semi-official one in the form of Liebknecht's sheet." (*Marx-Engels Collected Works*, 43:544). In a letter to Marx of July 10, 1869, Engels wrote, "It will be far more difficult to get rid of the South-German-republican-philistine narrow-mindedness drummed into the workers by Liebknecht. Just take the stupidity of inscribing on his sheet 'Organ of the People's Party'! If Bebel only had some theoretical knowledge, something like this could not happen; he seems to me to be a quite capable fellow, who simply has this one shortcoming." (*Collected Works*, 43:313). Marx nevertheless continued to work closely with Bebel and Liebknecht; a founder of a new continent of thought does not get to choose whom history brings to him.

24 Hermann Lueer, *Fundamental Principles of Communist Production and Distribution* (Hamburg: Red and Black Books, 2018), 13.

25 For a fuller discussion of Marx's concept of organization, see Peter Hudis, "Political Organization," in *The Marx Revival: Key Concepts and New Interpretations*, ed. Marcello Musto (Cambridge: Cambridge University Press, 2020), 108–25.

26 For a more extended critique of Lenin on this point, see Peter Hudis, "Imagining Society Beyond *Capital*," 181–99, in *Reading 'Capital' Today*, eds. Ingo Schmidt and Carlo Fanelli (London: Pluto Press, 2017).

27 See "Teaching of Economics in the Soviet Union," *American Economic Review*, September 1944. See also the critical responses to Dunayevskaya's "A New Revision of Marxian Economic" by Paul Baran, Oskar Lange, and Leo Rogin, as well as her "Revision or Reaffirmation of Marxism? A Rejoinder?" in the December 1944, March 1945, and September 1945 issues of the *American Economic Review.* Lange, who was teaching at the University of Chicago at the time, flew to Moscow in 1945, where he personally briefed Stalin about the controversy that this set off in the US.

28   See Group of International Communists, *Fundamental Principles of Communist Production and Distribution* (Hamburg: Red and Black Books, 2020). This should not be confused with Lueer's book of the same title, which serves as its introduction. A striking sign of the virtual complete disregard of the *Critique of the Gotha Program* in the decades after its composition is that the authors admit they did not even know of its existence when they began research for their study (see especially 171–72).

29   Raya Dunayevskaya, "The Theory of State-Capitalism: The Soviet Union as Capitalist Society," in *Against Capital in the Twenty-First Century*, eds. John Asimakopoulos and Richard Gilman-Opalsky (Philadelphia: Temple University Press, 2018), 49–50.

30   Frederick Engels, "Critique of the Draft Social-Democratic Program of 1891," in *Marx-Engels Collected Works* (New York: International Publishers, 1990), 7:224.

31   Group of International Communists, *Fundamental Principles of Communist Production and Distribution*, 178.

32   "A History of Separation," *Endnotes* no. 4 (October 2015): 185–86.

33   This is not to suggest that their interpretation is solely the result of misreading Marx's text. No less important (and perhaps the *reason* it misreads his text) is that *Endnotes* contends that the working class can no longer overcome capitalism since it has become highly fragmented and atomized. This is an inevitable result, they argue, of the logic of capital, which in displacing living labor from the process of production leads to the "abolition" of labor. Since "labor," as they see it, comes to an end with capitalism, Marx's discussion of labor time as a measure is interpreted to mean the principles of the old society define his discussion of the lower phase of the new society as well.

34   Tian Yu Cao, "Marx's Ideas and Conceptions of Socialism in the Twenty-First Century," in *Karl Marx's Life, Ideas, and Influences: A Critical Examination on the Bicentenary*, eds. Shaibal Gupta, Marcello Musto, and Babak Amini (Basingate: Palgrave Macmillan, 2019), 276.

35   *Grundrisse*, in *Marx-Engels Collected Works*, 29:91.

36   Perhaps the foremost expression of this is Moishe Postone's *Time, Labor, and Social Domination: A Reinterpretation of Marx's Critical Theory*. Postone sought to "free" Marx's critique of capital from any referent to a human subject that could uproot the system from within, on the grounds that class struggle does not negate the law of value but rather validates it. This is because, he contends, labor can serve as a social form of mediation only if concrete labor is subsumed by abstract labor. As he sees it, "labor" is not outside the value form of mediation but is inseparable from it. A postcapitalist society according to Postone therefore ipso facto involves the abolition of labor. For Postone, *dead labor* is the emancipatory alternative. His work completely ignores the *Critique of the Gotha Program*. For more on this, see Peter Hudis, "The Death of the Death of the Subject," in *Historical Materialism* 12, no. 3 (January 2004): 146–68.

37   For an approach that tries to rethink current prospects for revolution in light of the critical turning point reached with the movement for Black

lives and against police abuse that erupted in the spring and summer of 2020, see Peter Hudis, "The Seeds of Revolution Have Sprouted: What Is Now to Be Done?," *International Marxist-Humanist*, August 6, 2020, https://imhojournal.org/articles/the-seeds-of-revolution-have-sprouted-what-is-now-to-be-done.

38 Given the difference between the *Grundrisse* and *Capital*, it is understandable that advocates of the abolition of labor prefer the former over the latter. While everyone has the right to their opinion, it is always best to give greater weight to a thinker's later published and mature discussion of an issue when an apparent discrepancy exists with an earlier articulation of it. This especially important when it comes to Marx, who never ceased questioning, critiquing, and further developing his ideas and formulations.

39 *Capital*, I:667

40 *Capital*, I:290.

41 It is precisely this factor, I would argue, that explains why so few radical intellectuals have taken Marx's *Critique* as their ground—since grasping the depth of the divide between capitalism and socialism depends on acknowledging that ordinary people are fully capable of managing their affairs without statist or market forms of domination. This is something relatively few intellectuals are inclined to do.

42 Karl Marx, *The Ethnological Notebooks*, transcribed and edited by Lawrence Krader (Assen: Van Gorcum, 1972), 329.

43 Michael Lebowitz, *The Socialist Alternative: From Gotha to Now* (New York: Monthly Review Press, 2015), 71.

44 *Capital*, I:171.

45 Lueer, *Fundamental Principles of Communist Production and Distribution*, 11.

Critique of the Gotha Program

Note on the Translation

This translation by Kevin B. Anderson and Karel Ludenhoff
of Marx's *Critique of the Gotha Program* (1875) is based on the
German original in the *Marx-Engels Gesamtausgabe* (MEGA),
vol. I/25 (Berlin: Dietz Verlag, 1985). The MEGA, 122 volumes
projected, is the most comprehensive edition of the writings on
Marx and Engels, more than twice the size of the *Marx-Engels
Collected Works* (*MECW*). We have also consulted the anony-
mous translation in *MECW*, vol. 24 (London: 1989) and Terrell
Carver's translation in his edition of Marx's *Later Political Writings*
(Cambridge: Cambridge University Press, 1996). In addition, we
have translated into English for the first time the version of the
brief 1875 "Program of the Socialist Workers' Party of Germany
[Gotha Program]" that was the object of Marx's *Critique*. The
German original we used for the Gotha Program itself was also
from MEGA I/25.

Program of the Socialist Workers' Party of Germany [Gotha Program][1]

Gotha, May 1875

I. Labor is the source of all wealth and all culture, and since useful labor is possible only in society and through society, the proceeds of labor belong undiminished with equal right to all members of society.

In present-day society, the instruments of labor are the monopoly of the capitalist class; the corresponding subjection of the working class is the cause of all forms of misery and servitude.

The emancipation of labor demands the elevation of the instruments of labor into the common stock [*Gemeingut*[2]] of society and the cooperative regulation of the total labor, with fair distribution of the same.

The emancipation of labor must be the work of the working class, in relation to which all other classes are only one reactionary mass.

The working class strives for its emancipation first of all within the framework of the present-day national states, conscious that the necessary result of its efforts, which are common to the workers of all civilized countries, will be the international brotherhood of peoples.

II. Starting from these basic principles, the German Workers' Party strives by all legal means for the free state and a socialist society: the abolition of the wage system together with the iron law of wages and exploitation in every form; the elimination of all social and political inequality.

III. The German Workers' Party, in order *to pave the way to the solution of the social question,* demands the establishment of producers' cooperative societies *with state aid under the democratic control of the working people.* The producers' cooperative societies *are to be called into being* for industry and agriculture on such a scale *that the socialist organization of the total labor will arise from them.*

The German Workers' Party demands as the free basis of the state:

1) Universal, equal, and direct suffrage, with a secret ballot, for all men from twenty-one years old, for all state and local elections.
2) Direct legislation by the people and its right to propose and oppose legislation.
3) Universal military service, a people's army in place of the standing army. Questions of war and peace to be decided by parliament.
4) Abolition of all laws of exception, especially regarding the press, association and assembly.
5) Administration of justice by the people. Justice free of charge.

The German Workers' Party demands as the intellectual and ethical basis of the state:

1) Universal and equal elementary education of the people by the State. Universal compulsory school attendance. Free instruction.
2) Freedom of science. Freedom of conscience.

The German Workers' Party demands as the economic foundation of the state:
A single progressive income tax for the state and municipalities in place of all existing taxes, especially indirect ones.

The German Worker's Party demands, for the protection of the working class against the power of capital within present-day society:

1) Right of combination [*Coalitionsfreiheit*].[3]
2) A normal working day and prohibition of Sunday work.
3) Restriction of female labor and prohibition of child labor.
4) State supervision of factories, workshops, and home industries.
5) Regulation of prison labor.
6) An effective liability law.

Letter by Karl Marx to Wilhelm Bracke

London, May 5, 1875

Dear Bracke,

When you have read the following critical marginal notes on the Unity Program,[4] would you be so good as to send them on to Geib and Auer, Bebel and Liebknecht for examination.[5] *Notabene. The manuscript should be returned to you*, so as to be at my disposal if need be. I am exceedingly busy and have to overstep by far the limitations on work imposed on me by the doctors. Hence, it was anything but a "pleasure" to write such a lengthy screed. It was, however, necessary so that the steps to be taken by me later on would not be misinterpreted by our friends in the party for whom this communication is intended.

After the Unity Congress is finished, Engels and I will publish a short statement to the effect that we completely disassociate ourselves from said program's principles and have nothing to do with it.

This is indispensable because the opinion, an entirely erroneous one, is held abroad and assiduously nurtured by enemies of the party that we secretly guide from here the movement of the so-called Eisenach Party.[6] In a Russian book [*Statism and Anarchy*] that has recently appeared, Bakunin[7] still makes me responsible, for example, not only for all the programs, etc., of that party but even for every step taken by Liebknecht from the day of his cooperation with the People's Party.[8]

Apart from this, it is my duty not to give recognition, even by diplomatic silence, to what, according to my convictions, is a thoroughly objectionable program that is demoralizing for the party.[9]

Every step of real movement is more important than a dozen programs. If, therefore, it was not possible—and the circumstances of the time precluded this—to go *beyond* the Eisenach program, one should simply have concluded an agreement for action against the common enemy. But by drawing up a program of principles (instead of postponing this until it had been prepared for by a considerable period of common activity) one sets up before the whole world guideposts by which to measure the party's level of progress.

The Lassallean leaders came because circumstances forced this upon them.[10] If they had been told in advance that there would be no haggling about principles, they would *have had* to be content with a program of action or a plan of organization for common action. Instead of this, one permits them to arrive armed with mandates, recognizes these mandates on one's part as binding, and thus surrenders unconditionally to those who are themselves in need of help. To crown the whole business, they are holding a congress *before the Congress of Compromise*, while one's own party is holding its congress *post festum*. Obviously, their idea was to avoid all criticism and to give their own party no opportunity for reflection. One knows that the mere fact of unification is satisfying to the workers, but it is a mistake to believe that this momentary success is not bought too dearly.

Moreover, the program is no good, even apart from its canonization of the Lassallean articles of faith.

I shall be sending you in the near future the last installments of the French edition of *Capital*.[11] The printing was held up for a considerable time by a ban on the part of the French government. The thing will be ready this week or the beginning of next week. Have you received the previous six installments? Please let me have the address of Bernhard Becker,[12] to whom I must also send the final installments.

The *bookshop* of the *Volkstaat* has peculiar ways of doing things. Up to this moment, for example, I have not been sent a single copy of their reprint of the *Cologne Communist Trial*.[13]

With best regards,
Yours,
Karl Marx

Critique of the Gotha Program

I

1. "Labor is the source of all wealth and all culture, and since useful labor is possible only in society and through society, the proceeds of labor belong undiminished with equal right to all members of society."[14]

First part of the paragraph: "Labor is the source of all wealth and all culture."

Labor is *not the source* of all wealth. *Nature* is just as much the source of use values (and it is surely of such that material wealth consists?) as labor, which itself is only the manifestation of a force of nature, human labor power. The above phrase is to be found in all children's primers and is correct insofar as it is *implied* that labor is performed with the pertinent objects and instruments. But a socialist program cannot allow such bourgeois phrases to pass over in silence the *circumstances* that alone give them meaning. Only insofar as the human being from the beginning behaves toward nature, the primary source of all objects and instruments of labor [*Arbeitsmittel*[15]], as an owner, treats her as belonging to him, his labor becomes the source of use values, therefore also of wealth. The bourgeois have very good grounds for falsely ascribing *supernatural creative power* to labor, since it follows precisely from labor's dependance on nature that workers with no other property than their labor power must, in all conditions of society and culture, be the slave of other human beings who have made themselves the owners of the material conditions of labor. He can only work by their permission and hence only live with their permission.

Let us now leave the sentence as it stands, or rather limps. What could one have expected in conclusion? Obviously, this:

"Since labor is the source of all wealth, no one in society can appropriate wealth except as the product of labor. Therefore, if he himself does not work, he lives by the labor of others and also acquires his culture at the expense of the labor of others."

Instead of this, by means of the verbal river "and since," a proposition is added in order to draw a conclusion from this proposition and not from the first one.

Second part of the paragraph: "**Useful labor is possible only in society and through society.**"

According to the first proposition, labor was the source of all wealth and all culture; therefore, no society is possible without labor. Now we learn, conversely, that no "useful" labor is possible without society.

One could just as well have said that only in society can useless and even socially harmful labor become a branch of gainful occupation, that only in society can one live by being idle, etc., etc.—in short, one could just as well have copied the whole of Rousseau.[16]

And what is "useful" labor? Surely only labor that produces the intended useful result. A savage—and the human being was a savage after he had ceased to be an ape—who kills an animal with a stone, who collects fruit, etc., performs "useful" labor.

Thirdly, the conclusion: "**And because useful labor is possible only in society and through society, the proceeds of labor belong undiminished with equal right to all members of society.**"

A fine conclusion! If useful labor is possible only in society and through society, the proceeds of labor belong to society and only so much therefrom accrues to the individual worker as is not required to maintain the "condition [*Bedingung*[17]]" of labor, society.

In fact, this proposition has at all times been made use of *by the champions of the prevailing state of society at any given time.* First come the claims of the government and everything that sticks to it, since it is the social organ for the maintenance of the social order; then come the claims of the various kinds of private property owners, for the various kinds of private property are the foundations of society, etc. One sees that such hollow phrases can be twisted and turned as desired.

The first and second parts of the paragraph have some intelligible connection only in the following wording:

"Labor becomes the source of wealth and culture only as social labor," or, what is the same thing, "in and through society."

This proposition is indisputably correct, for although isolated labor (its material conditions presupposed) can create use value, it can create neither wealth nor culture.

But this other proposition is equally indisputable:

"In proportion as labor develops socially, and becomes thereby a source of wealth and culture, poverty and destitution develop among the workers, and wealth and culture among the nonworkers."

This is the law of all history hitherto. What, therefore, had to be done here, instead of generalizing about "labor" and "society," was to prove concretely how in contemporary capitalist society the material, etc., conditions have at last been created that enable and compel the workers to lift this historical curse.

In fact, however, the whole paragraph, bungled in style and content, is only there in order to inscribe the Lassallean catchword of the "undiminished proceeds of labor" as a slogan at the top of the party banner. I shall return later to the "proceeds of labor," "equal right," etc., since the same thing recurs in a somewhat different form further on.

2. **"In present-day society, the instruments of labor are the monopoly of the capitalist class; the resulting dependence of the working class is the cause of all forms of misery and servitude."**

This sentence, borrowed from the Rules of the International, is incorrect in this "improved" edition.[18]

In present-day society, the instruments of labor are the monopoly of the landowners (the monopoly of property in land is the very basis of the monopoly of capital) *and* the capitalists. In the passage in question, the Rules of the International do not mention either one or the other class of monopolists. They speak of the *"monopoly of the instruments of labor, that is, the sources of life."* That addition, "sources of life," makes it sufficiently clear that land is included in the instruments of labor.

The improvement was introduced because Lassalle, for reasons now generally known, attacked *only* the capitalist class and not the landowners. In England, the capitalist is usually not even the owner of the land on which his factory stands.

3. **"The emancipation of labor demands the elevation of the instruments of labor to the common stock of society and the cooperative regulation of the total labor, with a fair distribution of the proceeds of labor."**

"Elevation of the instruments of labor to the common stock." Ought obviously to read their "transformation into the common stock." But this only in passing.

What are the *"proceeds of labor"*? The product of labor or its value? And in the latter case, is it the total value of the product or only that part of the value that labor has added anew to the value of the means of production being consumed?

"Proceeds of labor" is a loose notion that Lassalle has put in the place of definite economic conceptions.

What is "a fair distribution"?

Do not the bourgeois assert that the present-day distribution is "fair"? And is it not, in fact, the only "fair" distribution on the basis of the present-day mode of production? Are economic relations regulated by legal concepts, or do not, on the contrary, legal relations arise out of economic ones? Don't the socialist sectarians also have the most varied notions about "fair" distribution?

To understand what is implied in this connection by the phrase "fair distribution," we must take the first paragraph and this one together. The latter presupposes a society wherein "the instruments of labor are common property and the total labor is cooperatively regulated," and from the first paragraph we learn that "the proceeds of labor belong undiminished with equal right to all members of society."

"To all members of society"? To those who do not work as well? What remains then of "the undiminished proceeds of labor"? Only to those members of society who work? What remains then of the "equal right" of all members of society?

But "all members of society" and "equal right" are obviously mere phrases. The kernel consists in this, that in this communist society every worker must receive the "undiminished" Lassallean "proceeds of labor."

Let us take, first of all, the words "proceeds of labor" in the sense of the product of labor; then the cooperative proceeds of labor are the *total social product*.

From this must now be deducted: *First*, cover for replacement of the means of production used up. *Second*, additional portion for expansion of production. *Third*, reserve or insurance funds to provide against accidents, dislocations caused by natural calamities, etc.

These deductions from the "undiminished" proceeds of labor are an economic necessity, and their magnitude is to be determined according to available means and forces, and partly by computation of probabilities, but they are in no way calculable by principles of justice.

There remains the other part of the total product, intended to serve as means of consumption.

Before this is divided among the individuals, there has to be deducted again, from it: *First*, the general costs of administration not belonging directly to production. This part will, from the outset, be very considerably restricted in comparison with present-day society, and it diminishes in proportion as the new society develops. *Second, that which is intended for the common satisfaction of needs*, such as schools, health services, etc. From the outset, this part grows considerably in comparison with present-day society, and it grows in proportion as the new society develops. *Third, funds for those unable to work*, etc., in short, for what is included under so-called official poor relief today.

Only now do we come to the "distribution" that the program, under Lassallean influence, alone has in view in its narrow fashion, namely, to that part of the means of consumption that is divided among the individual producers of the cooperative society [*Genossenschaft*].[19]

The "undiminished proceeds of labor" have already unnoticeably become converted into the "diminished" proceeds, although what the producer is deprived of in his capacity as a private individual benefits him directly or indirectly in his capacity as a member of society.

Just as the phrase concerning the "undiminished" proceeds of labor has disappeared, so now does the phrase "proceeds of labor" disappear altogether.

Within a cooperatively organized society based on common ownership of the means of production, the producers do not exchange their products; just as little does the labor expended on the products appear here *as the value* of these products, as a material quality possessed by them, since now, in contrast to capitalist society, individual labor no longer exists in an indirect fashion but directly as a component part of total labor. The phrase "proceeds of labor," objectionable also today on account of its ambiguity, thus loses all meaning.

Here we are dealing with a communist society, not as it has *developed* on its own foundations, but, on the contrary, just as it *emerges* from capitalist society; which is thus in every respect, economically, morally, and intellectually, still stamped with the birthmarks of the old society from whose womb it emerges.

Accordingly, the individual producer receives back from society, after the deductions have been made, exactly what he gives to it. What he has given to it is his individual quantum of labor. For example, the social working day consists of the sum of the individual hours of work; the individual labor time of the individual producer is the part of the social working day contributed by him, his share in it. He receives a certificate from society that he has furnished such-and-such an amount of labor (after deducting his labor for the common funds), and with this certificate, he draws from the societal supply [*gesellschaftlichen Vorrath*[20]] of means of consumption as much as the same amount of labor cost. The same amount of labor that he has given to society in one form, he receives back in another.

Here, obviously, the same principle prevails as that which regulates the exchange of commodities, insofar as this is exchange involving equal worth [*Gleichwertiger*].[21] Content and form are changed, because under the altered circumstances no one can give anything except his labor, and because, on the other hand, nothing can pass to the ownership of individuals, except individual means of consumption. But as far as the distribution of the latter among the individual producers is concerned, the same principle prevails as in the exchange of commodity equivalents: a given amount of labor in one form is exchanged for an equal amount of labor in another form.

Hence, *equal right* here is still in principle *bourgeois right*, although principle and practice are no longer at loggerheads, while the exchange of equivalents in commodity exchange exists only *on the average* and not in the individual case.

In spite of this advance, this *equal right* is still constantly encumbered by a bourgeois limitation. The right of the producers is *proportional* to the labor they supply; the equality consists in measurement that is made with an *equal standard*, labor. But one person is superior to another physically or mentally, and supplies more labor in the same time, or can labor for a longer time; and labor, to serve as a measure, must be defined by its duration or intensity, otherwise it ceases to be a standard of measurement. This *equal* right is an unequal right for unequal labor. It recognizes no class differences, because everyone is only a worker like everyone else; but it tacitly recognizes unequal individual endowment, and thus productive capacity of the workers, as a natural privilege. *It is, therefore, a right of inequality, in its content, like every right.* A right, by its very nature, can consist only in the application of an equal standard; but unequal individuals (and they would not be different individuals if they were not unequal) are measurable only by an equal standard insofar as they are brought under an equal criterion, grasped only in terms of a specific aspect, for instance, in the present case, are regarded *only as workers* and nothing more is seen in them, everything else being ignored. Moreover, one worker is married, another is not; one has more children than another, and so on and so forth. Thus, with equal labor productivity, and hence an equal share in the social consumption fund, one will in fact receive more than another, one will be richer than another, etc. To avoid all these defects, rights would have to be unequal rather than equal.

But these defects are inevitable in the first phase of communist society as it is when it has just emerged after prolonged birth pangs from capitalist society. Right can never be higher than the economic form of society and the cultural development conditioned [*bedingte*[22]] by it.

In a higher phase of communist society, after the enslaving subordination of the individual to the division of labor, and thereby also the antithesis between mental and physical labor, has vanished; after labor has become not only a means of life but life's prime desire and necessity [*erste Lebensbedürfniss*[23]]; after the productive forces have also increased with the all-round development of the individual, and all the springs of cooperative wealth flow more abundantly, only then can the narrow horizon of bourgeois right be completely transcended [*überschritten*[24]] and society inscribe on its banners: From each according to his abilities, to each according to his needs!

I have dealt at greater length with the "undiminished" proceeds of labor, on the one hand, and with "equal right" and "fair distribution," on the other, in order to show what an outrage it is to attempt, on the one hand, to force on our party again, as dogmas, ideas that in a certain period had some meaning but have now become obsolete verbal rubbish, while again perverting, on the other, the realistic outlook that it cost so much effort to instill in the party but that has now taken root in it, by means of ideological nonsense about right and other nonsense common among the democrats and French socialists.[25]

Quite apart from the analysis so far given, it was in general a mistake to make a fuss about so-called *distribution* and put the principal stress on it.

At any given time, the distribution of the means of consumption is only a consequence of the distribution of the conditions of production themselves. The latter distribution, however, is a feature of the mode of production itself. The capitalist mode of production, for example, rests on the material conditions of production being in the hands of nonworkers in the form of property in capital and land, while the masses are only owners of their personal prerequisites of production, of labor power. If the elements of production are so distributed, then the present-day distribution of the means of consumption results from this. If the material conditions of production are the cooperative property of the workers themselves, then there likewise results a distribution of the means of consumption different from the present one. Vulgar socialism (and from it in turn a section of the democrats) has taken over from the bourgeois economists the consideration and treatment of distribution as independent of the mode of production and hence the presentation of socialism as turning principally on distribution. After the real relation has long been made clear, why retrogress again?

4. "**The emancipation of labor must be the work of the working class, in relation to which all other classes are** *only one reactionary mass.*"

The first clause is taken from the introduction to the Rules of the International, but "improved." There it is said: "The emancipation of the working class must be conquered by the workers themselves";[26] here, on the contrary, the "working class" has to emancipate—what? "Labor." Let him understand who can.

In compensation, the subordinate clause, on the other hand, is a Lassallean quotation of the purest sort: "in relation to which (the working class) all other classes are *only one reactionary mass.*"

In the *Communist Manifesto* it is stated: "Of all the classes that stand face-to-face with the bourgeoisie today, the proletariat alone is a *really revolutionary class.* The other classes decay and finally disappear in the face of Modern Industry; the proletariat is its characteristic [*eigenstes*] product."[27]

The bourgeoisie is here conceived as a revolutionary class, as the bearer of large-scale industry in relation to the feudal lords and the "lower middle class" [*Mittelständen*],[28] who desire to maintain all the social positions that are the creation of obsolete modes of production. Thus, these classes do not form *together with the bourgeoisie* merely one reactionary mass.

On the other hand, the proletariat is revolutionary in relation to the bourgeoisie because, having itself emerged on the basis of large-scale industry, it strives to strip off from production the capitalist character that the bourgeoisie seeks to perpetuate. But the *Manifesto* adds that the "lower middle classes (become) revolutionary ... in view of their impending transfer into the proletariat."[29]

From this point of view, therefore, it is again nonsense to say that they, "together with the bourgeoisie," and with the feudal lords into the bargain, "form only one reactionary mass" in relation to the working class.

Did we proclaim to the artisans, small manufacturers, etc., and *peasants* during the last elections: In relation to us, you, together with the bourgeoisie and feudal lords, form one reactionary mass?

Lassalle knew the *Communist Manifesto* by heart, as his faithful followers know the gospels written by him. If, therefore, he has falsified it so grossly, this has occurred only to gloss over his alliance with absolutist and feudal opponents against the bourgeoisie.

In the above paragraph, moreover, his oracular saying is dragged in without any connection to the botched quotation from the Rules of the International. Thus, it is here simply an impertinence, and indeed not at all displeasing to Herr Bismarck, one of those cheap pieces of insolence in which the Marat of Berlin deals.[30]

5. "**The working class strives for its emancipation first of all** *within the framework of the present-day national state*, **conscious that the necessary result of its efforts, which are common to the workers of all civilized countries, will be the international brotherhood of peoples.**"

Lassalle, in opposition to the *Communist Manifesto* and to all earlier socialism, conceived the workers' movement from the narrowest national standpoint. Here he is being followed, and this after the work of the International!

It is altogether self-evident that, to be able to fight at all, the working class must organize itself at home *as a class* and that its own country is the immediate arena of its struggle insofar as its class struggle is national, not in substance but, as the *Communist Manifesto* states, "in form."[31] But the "framework of the present-day national state," for instance, the German Empire, is itself, in its turn, economically within the "framework of the world market," politically within the "framework of the system of states." Every businessman knows that German trade is at the same time foreign trade, and the greatness of Herr Bismarck consists, to be sure, precisely in pursuing this kind of *international* policy.

And to what does the German Workers' Party reduce its internationalism? To the consciousness that the result of its efforts "will be the *international brotherhood of peoples*," a phrase borrowed from the bourgeois League of Peace and Freedom,[32] which is intended to pass as equivalent to the international brotherhood of working classes in the joint struggle against the ruling classes and their governments. Not a word, therefore, *about the international functions* of the German working class! And it is thus that it is to challenge its own bourgeoisie, which is already linked up in brotherhood against it with the bourgeois of all other countries, and Herr Bismarck's international intrigues!

In fact, the commitment to internationalism of the program stands *infinitely below even* that of the free trade party. The latter also asserts that the result of its efforts will be "the international brotherhood of peoples." But it also *does* something to make trade international and by no means contents itself with the consciousness that all people are carrying on trade at home.

The international activity of the working classes does not in any way depend on the existence of the "International Working Men's Association." This was only the first attempt to create a central organ for that activity; an attempt that was a lasting success on account of the impetus that it gave, but which was no longer realizable *in its first historical form* after the fall of the Paris Commune.

Bismarck's *Norddeutsche*[33] was absolutely right when it announced, to the satisfaction of its master, that the German Workers' Party had sworn off internationalism in the new program.

II

"Starting from these basic principles, the German Workers' Party strives by all legal means for the *free state—and—*the socialist society: the abolition of the wage system *together with the iron law of wages* and exploitation in every form; the elimination of all social and political inequality."

I shall return to the "free" state later.

So, in future, the German Workers' Party has got to believe in Lassalle's "iron law of wages"![34] That this may not be lost, the nonsense is perpetrated of speaking of the "abolition of the wage system" (it should read: system of wage labor) *"together with* the iron law of wages." If I abolish wage labor, then naturally I abolish its laws also, whether they are of "iron" or sponge. But Lassalle's attack on wage labor turns almost solely on this so-called law. In order, therefore, to prove that Lassalle's sect has conquered, the "wage system" must be abolished *"together with* the iron law of wages" and not without it.

It is well known that nothing of the "iron law of wages" is Lassalle's except the word "iron" borrowed from Goethe's "great, eternal iron laws."[35] The word *iron* is his sign, by which the true believers recognize one another. But if I take the law with Lassalle's stamp on it, and consequently in his sense, then I must also take it with his explanation. And what is that? As Lange already showed, shortly after Lassalle's death, it is the Malthusian theory of population (preached by Lange himself).[36] But if this theory is correct, then again I cannot abolish the law even if I abolish wage labor a hundred times over, because the law then governs not only the system of wage labor but *every* social system. Basing themselves directly on this, the economists have been proving for fifty years and more that socialism cannot abolish poverty, *which has its basis in nature*, but can only make it *general*, distributing it simultaneously over the whole surface of society!

But all this is not the main thing. *Quite apart* from the *false* Lassallean formulation of the law, the truly outrageous retrogression consists in the following:

Since Lassalle's death, there has asserted itself in our party the scientific understanding that *wages* are not what they *appear* to be, namely the *value of labor with respect to its price,* but only a masked form for the *value of labor power with respect to its price.*[37] Thereby, the whole earlier bourgeois conception of wages, as well as all the earlier criticism directed against this conception, was thrown overboard once and for all. It was made clear that the wage worker has permission to work for his own subsistence, that is, *to live*, only insofar as he works for a certain time without pay for the capitalist (and hence also for the latter's co-consumers of surplus value); that the whole capitalist system of production turns on the increase of this unpaid labor by extending the working day, or by developing productivity, that is, increasing the intensity of labor power, etc.; that, consequently, the system of wage labor is a system of slavery, and indeed of a slavery that becomes proportionally more severe as the social productive forces of labor develop, whether the payment the worker receives is better or worse. And after this understanding has gained more and more ground in our party, they return to Lassalle's dogma although they must have known that Lassalle *did not know* what wages were, but, following in the wake of the bourgeois economists, took the appearance for the essence of the matter.

It is as if, among slaves who have finally gotten out from under the secret of slavery and broken out in rebellion, a slave still in thrall to obsolete notions were to inscribe on the program of the rebellion: Slavery must be abolished because the feeding and lodging of slaves in the system of slavery cannot surpass a certain low level!

Does not the mere fact that the representatives of our party were capable of perpetrating such a monstrous attack on the understanding that has spread among the mass of our party prove, by itself, with what criminal levity and with what lack of conscience they set to work in drawing up this compromise program!

Instead of the indefinite concluding phrase of the paragraph, "the elimination of all social and political inequality," it ought to have been said that with the abolition of class distinctions all social and political inequality arising from them would disappear of itself.

III

"The German Workers' Party, in order to *pave the way to the solution of the social question*, demands the establishment of producers' cooperative societies *with state aid under the demo-cratic control of the working people*. The producers' cooperative societies *are to be called into being* for industry and agriculture on such a scale *that the socialist organization of the total labor will arise from them*."

After the Lassallean "iron law of wages," the panacea of the prophet! The way to it is "paved" in worthy fashion. In place of the existing class struggle appears a newspaper scribbler's phrase: "*the* social *question*," for the "*solution*" of which one "paves the way."

Instead of arising from the revolutionary process of transformation of society, the "socialist organization of the total labor" "arises" from the "state aid" that the state gives to the producers' cooperative societies, which the *state*, not the workers, "*calls into being*." It is worthy of Lassalle's imagination that with state loans one can build a new society as easily as a new railway!

From the remnants of a sense of shame, "state aid" has been put "under the democratic control of the working people."

In the first place, the majority of the "working people" in Germany consists of peasants, not proletarians.

Second, "democratic" means in German "by the rule of the people [*volksherrschaftlich*]." But what does "control of the working people by the rule of the people" mean? And particularly in the case of working people who, through these demands that they put to the state, exhibit a clear consciousness that they neither rule nor are ready to do so!

It would be superfluous to deal here with the criticism of the recipe prescribed by Buchez in the reign of Louis Philippe, in *opposition* to the French socialists and accepted by the reactionary workers of *L'Atelier*.[38] The chief offense does not lie in having inscribed this specific miracle cure in the program, but in taking a generally retrograde step, from the standpoint of a class movement to that of a sectarian one.

That the workers desire to establish the conditions for cooperative production on a social scale, and first of all on a national scale, in their own country, only means that they are working to overthrow the present conditions of production, and it has nothing in common with the foundation of cooperative societies with state aid. But as far as the present cooperative societies are concerned, they are of value *only* insofar as they are the independent creations of the workers and not protégés of either the government or the bourgeoisie.

IV

I come now to the democratic section.

A. *"The free basis of the state."*

First of all, according to II, the German Workers' Party strives for "the free state."

Free state—what is this?

It is by no means the aim of the workers, who have got rid of the narrow mentality of humble subjects, to set the state "free." In the German Empire, the "state" is almost as "free" as in Russia. Freedom consists in converting the state from an organ superimposed upon society into one completely subordinate to it; and also today, the state formations [*Staatsformen*] are freer or less free to the extent that they restrict the "freedom of the state."

The German Workers' Party, at least if it adopts the program, shows that its socialist ideas are not even skin-deep, in that, instead of treating existing society (and this holds true for any future one) as the *basis* of the existing state (or of the future state in the case of a future society), it treats the state rather as an independent entity that possesses its own *"intellectual, ethical, and libertarian bases."*

And what wild abuse the program makes of the words *"present-day state," "present-day society,"* and of the even wilder misconception it creates in regard to the state to which it addresses its demands?

"Present-day society" is capitalist society, which exists in all civilized countries, more or less free from medieval admixture, more or less modified by the particular historical development of each country, more or less developed. On the other hand, the "present-day state" changes with a country's frontier. It is different in the Prusso-German Empire from what it is in Switzerland, and different in England from what it is in the United States. *"The* present-day state" is therefore a fiction.

Nevertheless, the different states of the different civilized countries, in spite of their multifarious diversity of form, all have this in common, that they are based on modern bourgeois society, more or less capitalistically developed. They have, therefore, also certain essential characteristics in common. In this sense, it is possible to speak of the "present-day" body politic [Staatswesen[39]] in contrast with the future, in which its present root, bourgeois society, will have died off.

The question then arises: What transformation will the body politic [Staatswesen] undergo in communist society? In other words, what social functions analogous to present state functions [Staatsfunktionen] will remain at that juncture? This question can only be answered scientifically, and one does not get a flea-hop nearer to the problem by a thousandfold combination of the word "people" with the word "state."

Between capitalist and communist society there lies the period of the revolutionary transformation of the one into the other. Corresponding to this is also a political transition period in which the state can be nothing but *the revolutionary dictatorship of the proletariat.*[40]

But the program deals neither with this nor with the future body politic [*Staatswesen*] of communist society.

Its political demands contain nothing beyond the old democratic litany familiar to all: universal suffrage, direct legislation, popular rights, a people's militia, etc. They are a mere echo of the bourgeois People's Party, of the League of Peace and Freedom. They are all demands that, insofar as they are not exaggerated in fantastic presentation, have already been *realized*. Only the state to which they belong does not lie within the borders of the German Empire, but in Switzerland, the United States, etc. This sort of "state of the future" is a *present-day state*, although existing outside the "framework" of the German Empire.

But one thing has been forgotten. Since the German Workers' Party expressly declares that it acts within "the present-day national state," hence within its own state, the Prusso-German Empire, its demands would indeed be otherwise largely meaningless, since one only demands what one has not got—it should not have forgotten the chief thing, namely, that all those pretty little things rest on the recognition of the so-called sovereignty of the people and hence are appropriate only in a *democratic republic*.

Since one has not the courage—and wisely so, for the circumstances demand caution[41]—to demand a democratic republic, as the French workers' programs under Louis Philippe and under Louis Napoleon[42] did, one should not have resorted, either, to the subterfuge, neither "honest"[43] nor decent, of demanding things that have meaning only in a democratic republic, from a state that is nothing but a police-guarded military despotism, embellished with parliamentary forms, alloyed with a feudal admixture, and at the same time already influenced by the bourgeoisie, and bureaucratically structured, and in addition to this to give assurances to this state that they think it will be possible to force such things upon it "by legal means."

Even vulgar democracy, which sees the millennium in the democratic republic, and has no suspicion that it is precisely in this last form of the state in bourgeois society that the class struggle has to be fought out to a conclusion, even it towers mountains above this kind of democratism, which keeps within the limits of what is permitted by the police and not permitted by logic.

That, in fact, by the word "state" is meant the government machine, or the state insofar as it forms a special organism separated from society through division of labor, is shown by the words "the German Workers' Party demands *as the economic basis of the state*: a single progressive income tax," etc. Taxes are the economic basis of the government machinery and of nothing else. In the state of the future, already existing in Switzerland, this demand has been pretty well fulfilled. An income tax presupposes various sources of income of the various social classes, and hence capitalist society. It is, therefore, nothing remarkable that the Liverpool financial reformers, bourgeois headed by Gladstone's brother,[44] are putting forward the same demand as the program.

B. "The German Workers' Party demands as the intellectual and ethical basis of the state:
1. Universal and *equal elementary education of the people* by the state. Universal compulsory school attendance. Free instruction."

"Equal elementary education of the people"? What idea lies behind these words? Is it believed that in present-day society (and it is only with this one is dealing) education can be *equal* for all classes? Or is it demanded that the upper classes also shall be compulsorily reduced to the modicum of education, the elementary school, which alone is compatible with the economic conditions not only of the wage workers but of the peasants as well?

"Universal compulsory school attendance. Free instruction." The former exists even in Germany, the second in Switzerland and in the United States in the case of elementary schools. If in some states of the latter country "upper" educational institutions are also "free," that only means in fact defraying the cost of education of the upper classes from the general tax receipts. Incidentally, the same holds good for "free administration of justice" demanded under A, 5. The administration of criminal justice is to be had free everywhere; that of civil justice is concerned almost exclusively with conflicts over property and hence affects almost exclusively the propertied classes. Are they to carry on their litigation at public expense?

This paragraph on the schools should at least have demanded technical schools (theoretical and practical) in combination with elementary schools.

"Elementary education by the state" is altogether objectionable. Defining by a general law the expenditures on the elementary schools, the qualifications of the teaching staff, the branches of instruction, etc., and, as is done in the United States, supervising the fulfillment of these legal specifications by state inspectors, is a very different thing from appointing the state as the educator of the people! Government and church should instead be equally excluded from any influence on the schools. Particularly, indeed, in the Prusso-German Empire (and one should not take refuge in the rotten subterfuge that one is speaking of a "state of the future"; we have seen how matters stand in this respect) the state has need, on the contrary, of a very stern education by the people.

But the whole program, despite its ring of democracy, is tainted through and through by the Lassallean sect's servile belief in the state, or, what is no better, a belief in democratic miracles; or rather it is a compromise between these two kinds of belief in miracles, both equally remote from socialism.

2. *"Freedom of science,"* says a paragraph of the Prussian Constitution. Why, then, here?

"Freedom of conscience"! If one desired, at this time of the *Kulturkampf*,[45] to remind liberalism of its old catchwords, it surely could have been done only in the following form: Everyone should be able to attend his religious as well as his bodily needs without the police sticking their noses in. But at any rate, the Workers' Party ought to have, in this connection, to have expressed its awareness that bourgeois "freedom of conscience" is nothing but the toleration of all possible kinds of *religious unfreedom of conscience*, and that for its part it endeavors rather to liberate the conscience from the ghostly apparitions of religion. But they choose not to transgress the "bourgeois" level.

I have now come to the end, for the appendix that now follows in the program does not constitute a *characteristic* component of it. Hence, I can be very brief.

Appendix

2. *"Normal working day."*

In no other country has the workers' party limited itself to such an indefinite demand, but has always fixed the length of the working day that it considers normal under the given circumstances.

3. **"Restriction of female labor and prohibition of child labor."**

The standardization of the working day must include the restriction of women's labor, insofar as it relates to the duration, intermissions, etc., of the working day; otherwise, it could only mean the exclusion of female labor from branches of industry that are especially unhealthy for the female body, or are morally objectionable for the female sex. If that is what was meant, it should have been said.

"Prohibition of child labor." Here it was absolutely essential to state the *age limit*.

A *general prohibition* of child labor is incompatible with the existence of large-scale industry and hence an empty, pious wish.

Its realization, if it were possible, would be reactionary, since with a strict regulation of the working time according to the different age groups and other safety measures for the protection of children, an early combination of productive labor with education is one of the most potent means for the transformation of present-day society.

4. **"State supervision of factories, workshops, and domestic industry."**

In consideration of the Prusso-German state, it should definitely have been demanded that the inspectors are to be removable only by a court of law; that any worker can have them prosecuted for neglect of duty; that they must belong to the medical profession.

5. **"Regulation of prison labor."**

A petty demand in a general workers' program. In any case, it should have been clearly stated that there is no intention from fear of competition to allow ordinary criminals to be treated like animals, and especially that there is no desire to deprive them of their sole means of betterment, productive labor. This was surely the least we could have expected from socialists.

6. **"An effective liability law."**

It should have been stated what is meant by an "effective" liability law.

Be it noted, incidentally, that, in speaking of the normal working day, the part of factory legislation that deals with health regulations and safety measures, etc., has been overlooked. The liability law comes into operation only when these regulations are infringed.

In short, this appendix also is distinguished by slovenly editing.

Dixi et salvavi animam meam [I have spoken and saved my soul].[46]

[While undated, the *Critique of the Gotha Program* was apparently written between the end of April and May 5, 1875.]

Notes

1   This draft version, the one to which Marx was responding, appeared on March 7, 1875, in the newspapers *Der Volkstaat* (Leipzig, organ of the Eisenachers) and *Neue Social-Demokrat* (Berlin, organ of the Lassalleans). The version we consulted is the one that has been republished in German in the *Marx-Engels Gesamtausgabe* I / 25 (Berlin: Dietz Verlag, 1985), 515–16. To our knowledge, this is the first English translation of the version of the Gotha Program to which Marx was responding.

2   Could also be translated as common goods / assets of society.

3   As in the right to organize trade unions and political parties.

4   "Programm der deutschen Arbeiterpartei [Program of the German Workers' Party]," *Der Volkstaat* no. 27, March 7, 1875, reproduced in this volume, 43–45. The official name of this group was the Sozialistische Arbeiterpartei Deutschlands [Socialist Workers' Party of Germany], but Marx refers to it in the *Critique* as the German Workers' Party, in keeping with the wording in the Gotha Program.

5   August Geib (1842–79), Ignaz Auer (1846–1907, later a reformist), August Bebel (1840–1913), and Wilhelm Liebknecht (1826–1900), along with the recipient of this letter, Wilhelm Bracke (1842–80), were leaders of the Social Democratic Workers' Party, known as the "Eisenach Party," due to its founding in Eisenach in 1869. Bebel and Liebknecht were to become important leaders of the Second International, founded in 1889, six years after Marx's death.

6   See previous note.

7   Mikhail Bakunin (1814–76), Russian revolutionary and major founder of what came to be called anarchism. Bakunin accused Marx of statism and elitism within the International Working Men's Association (First International). He also wanted the International to espouse political atheism and opposed its engagement with Irish national liberation.

8   The South German People's Party was a liberal anti-Prussian party with a small labor wing.

9   Here Marx is not referring to a specific organization but to those organizations that were guided by genuinely revolutionary principles and to

the theory underlying them, as in works like *Capital* or the *Communist Manifesto*. Sometimes "the party" referred to only Engels and himself.

10 Ferdinand Lassalle (1825–64), was a prominent German lawyer who became the leader of the General German Workers Federation, founded in 1863. Lassalle espoused a statist form of socialism that strongly influenced post-Marx Marxism, especially in Germany.

11 The 1872–75 French edition of *Capital*, vol. I, the last version of the book Marx saw through to publication, appeared in installments. Marx is sending it to his German followers because, as he wrote a week earlier (April 28) in the postface, "it possesses a scientific value independent of the German original and should be consulted even by readers familiar with German" (*Capital*, vol. I, trans. Ben Fowkes [New York: Penguin, 1976], 105).

12 Bernhard Becker (1826–82), German socialist active in the Eisenach Party.

13 Marx, *Revelations Concerning the Communist Trial in Cologne* (1853), a polemic against the repression of his comrades in the wake of the 1848 revolution.

14 These and subsequent quotations are from the Gotha Program.

15 "Instruments of labor [*Arbeitsmittel*]" could also be translated as "means of labor." In *Capital*, Marx's term is rendered this way in the most recent translation: "An instrument of labor [*Arbeitsmittel*] is a thing, or a complex of things, which the worker imposes between himself and the object of his labor and which serves as a conductor, directing his activity onto that object. He makes use of the mechanical, physical, and chemical properties of some substances as instruments of his power [*Machtmittel*], and in accordance with his purposes" (Marx, *Capital*, vol. I, trans. Ben Fowkes [New York: New Left Books, 1976], 284). These instruments or means of labor can thus include anything from tools and machines to land and water resources. The English phrase "means of labor" was apparently in wider use during Marx's time. Nowadays, the German term *Arbeitsmittel*, to which it corresponds, has usually been translated as "instruments of labor" or even "means of production." In this edition, we have used "instruments of labor," at variance with most other translations of the *Critique of the Gotha Program*.

16 Jean-Jacques Rousseau (1712–78), Franco-Swiss Enlightenment philosopher and liberal social contract theorist; posited a prepolitical "state of nature" marked by freedom and human solidarity; strongly influenced the French Revolution of 1789.

17 Could also be translated as "determinant" or "prerequisite."

18 According to the introduction, composed by Marx in English, to the 1866 Rules of the International Working Men's Association (First International): "That the economical subjection of the man of labor to the monopolizer of the means [instruments] of labor, that is, the sources of life, lies at the bottom of servitude in all its forms, of all social misery, mental degradation, and political dependence." *Marx-Engels Collected Works* (hereafter *MECW*), 20:441.

19 This could also be translated as "association" or "collective."

20 Could also be translated as "societal supplies" or "social stock."

21 Could also be translated as "equal values," "equal entities," or "what is equally estimable." However, we did not translate it as "value" because value production in the capitalist sense has ended as of this point.

22 This could also be translated as "determined."

23 The German word *Bedürfnis* carries the twin meanings of desire/wish and necessity/need. This phrase has sometimes been translated "life's prime want."

24 Literally, "crossed over."

25 The latter refers primarily to those influenced by Pierre-Joseph Proudhon (1809–65) and other leftist neo-Ricardians, who were the major force in French socialism during the nineteenth century. The reformist Federation of the Socialist Workers of France was formed later, in 1879, and the first putatively Marxist party, the French Workers Party, was founded in 1880.

26 *MECW*, 20:440.

27 *MECW*, 6:494, translation slightly altered on basis of German original.

28 This could also be translated as "middle estates" or "middle layers," but "lower middle class" is the translation used in most English editions of the *Communist Manifesto*.

29 *MECW*, 6:494.

30 Otto von Bismarck (1815–98), longtime chancellor under the Prussian (later German) Empire; Jean-Paul Marat (1742–93), a leader of the far-left *sans culottes* during the French Revolution; "Marat of Berlin" is an ironical reference to Wilhelm Hasselmann (1844–1916), editor of the Lassallean newspaper *Neuen Social-Demokraten*.

31 *MECW*, 6:495.

32 Large pacifist organization founded in Switzerland in 1867, which called for European unity. Some revolutionaries like Bakunin participated, but Marx blocked official adherence on the part of the International.

33 *Norddeutsche Allgemeine Zeitung,* conservative newspaper aligned with Bismarck.

34 Notion that even temporary improvements in wages were impossible under capitalism.

35 The German Romantic poet Johann Wolfgang Goethe (1749–1832) penned these lines in his hymn "Das Göttliche" ("On the Divine," 1785).

36 Thomas Malthus (1766–1834) was an English political economist and theologian who expounded the theory (Malthusianism) that a rising population would inevitably lead to poverty; ridiculed by Marx as a reactionary and confused in his thinking. Friedrich Albert Lange (1828–75) was a German neo-Kantian philosopher and a Lassallean, who wrote a history of materialism.

37 The distinction that Marx makes here between labor and labor power, or the *capacity* to labor, is one of his most important theoretical insights.

38 Louis Philippe, last French king (reign: 1830–48); Philippe Buchez (1796–1865) founder in 1840 of the Christian utopian socialist magazine, *L'Atelier* [The Workshop].

39 All previous English translations have rendered this word as "state" here and in the next sentence. However, the actual word Marx uses, *Staatswesen* (not *Staat*), refers to something far less definite, to the "body politic" (the political body of society) as we have rendered it here. *Staatswesen* could also be translated as "state functions" or very literally as "essence/underlying nature" of the state. In any case, it is something less definite or specific than "state." Note also that Marx uses a related term, *Staatsfunktionen* (state functions) two sentences later, which he links directly to *Staatswesen* by the phrase "in other words."

40 This has often been thought to refer to the revolutionary working-class direct democracy of the Paris Commune of 1871, at a time when most of the wealthier classes had fled the city.

41 It was illegal to call for a republic in the German Empire.

42 Louis Napoleon Bonaparte (Napoleon III) ruled France from 1851 to 1870 in what came to be known as the Bonapartist regime, the first modern police state.

43 "Honest" was the nickname of the Eisenachers, hence another dig at his German comrades.

44 The Liverpool Financial Reform Association, headed by Robertson Gladstone (1805–75), brother of the prominent Liberal politician William Gladstone (1809–98), advocated what it considered to be fair and equitable taxation upon both property and income.

45 The *Kulturkampf* (struggle over culture) was a campaign by Bismarck's government in the 1870s against Catholics, especially in the German-occupied portion of Poland, which was masked as a fight for secular culture and education.

46 Ezekiel 3:18–19.

Afterword to Karl Marx, *Critique of the Gotha Program*

To the memory of Noel Ignatiev

Dixi et salvavi animam meam. With these Latin words Karl Marx concludes his *Critique of the Gotha Program* (1875)—"I have spoken and saved my soul." One is unaccustomed to religious expression from the great communist, unless it be sarcastic, yet here he uses it to conclude a devastating analysis of the program of the German Workers' Party. What is Marx's soul? How did he save it? And what about ours?[1]

These Latin words from two and a half millennia previous were distilled from a "brazen and stubborn" prophet, Ezekiel, who with bizarre, way-out visions of animals, jewels, and wheels within wheels heard these words whispered from the heavenly vault:

> If I pronounce sentence of death on a wicked person and you have not warned him or spoken out to dissuade him from his wicked ways and so save his life, that person will die because of his sin, but I shall hold you answerable for his death. But if you have warned him and he persists in his wicked ways, he will die because of his sin, but you will have discharged your duty (Ezekiel 3:18–19 or 33:7–11).

Perhaps Marx learned this in childhood. The oracular voice and the prophetic role came easily to him. *Dixi et salvavi* was used by Engels too writing thirty years earlier in *The Condition of the Working Class in England* (1844) when it expressed bourgeois contempt. The phrase from Ezekiel became part of pompous boss-talk as the boss clears his conscience and walks away. And for a moment Marx and Engels considered walking away from the nascent German socialist party but hung on in there, despite Marx's criticisms. Marx, however, at this moment of obligation refers to capitalism and its wicked ways.

Salvation depends on speaking; it is the moral imperative. Black Lives Matter speaks truth to power; Extinction Rebellion's slogan is "to tell the truth"; and women in north America form "speak outs" in recovering from male violence. Indispensable to the revolutionary project is calling out the wicked ways. Black Lives Matter has pointed to the murderous effects of white supremacy. #MeToo has pointed to the violent degradations inherent to patriarchy. Extinction Rebellion has taken direct action against the political and economic causes of planetary warming. At Standing Rock indigenous people attempt to prevent pollution of the waters. Racism, patriarchy, settler colonialism, and destruction of the planetary earth system are the "wicked ways." These are four destructive structures of capitalism. With them in mind we look back to select what is useful from Marx's *Critique*, bearing in mind, so to speak, that Marx also looks to us!

Engels published (and revealed) the *Condition of the English Working Class* in 1844. That year too found Marx publishing an earlier "critique," not of a political program but of a political philosophy. *A Contribution to the Critique of Hegel's Philosophy of Right*, in which he described religion as "the sigh of the oppressed creature, the heart of a heartless world, and the soul of soulless conditions." "Criticism has plucked," he writes, "the imaginary flowers on the chain not in order that man shall continue to bear that chain without fantasy or consolation but so that he shall throw off the chain and pluck the living flower." To unmask self-estrangement he must turn to the criticism of actualities, and turn to history "to establish the truth of this world." The two revolutionaries, Marx and Engels, one a critical philosopher and the other an empirical investigator, formed a partnership as revolutionary communists.

A year or so later they write, "Communism is for us not a *state of affairs* which is to be established, an *ideal* to which reality [will] have to adjust itself. We call communism the *real* movement which abolishes the present state of things. The conditions of this movement result from the premises now in existence."[2] And that real movement in dissolving the world market abolishes alien property relations and restores mutual human relations. It is for us to see that *real* movement." Marx makes the point again in the *Critique of the Gotha Program*: "Every step of real movement is more important than a dozen programs."

The goal is the commons, the means is the proletariat. What did these words—commons, proletariat—actually mean to him or to us? How are they part of the "real movement which abolishes the present state of things"?

Instead of proletariat he will write of producers or labor power. He'll refer to serfs, to slaves; he'll include employed and unemployed (the active army, the reserve army); he'll refer to peasants, to artisans, to small manufacturers. All people who have lost their organic connections to nature, that is, to land, its creatures, its grains; to the waters and pastures; as well as to the geological resources lying beneath the land. All people from whom have been expropriated the means of life, the means of production, the means of subsistence, this is what he means. It only remains to organize! "It is altogether self-evident that to be able to fight at all the working class must organize itself at home *as a class*," he states in this *Critique*. Yet this "class" is constantly changing in its composition.

By the 1860s as the workers' movement revived after the defeats that followed 1848, socialist parties were formed in Germany, and Marx helped to organize in 1864 the International Working Men's Association, or the First International. It culminated with the Paris Commune of 1871, two months of self-rule by the French working class, the first proletarian revolution.

The Gotha Program says that labor is the source of all wealth. No, it's not, says Marx. Nature is just as much a source of material wealth as labor. The single negation, right at the beginning with the little word "no" is the key that opens the door, for us in the twenty-first century, to planetary warming and the sixth extinction. We walk right in with the ecosocialism of Joel Kovel, Michael Löwy, and John Foster Bellamy.[3] We are present at the edge of the abyss staring into the "ecological rift." Marx wrote of the "irreparable break" between nature and society. Or he'd call the nature-humanity relation "metabolism." The mass slaughter of the bison, the deforestation of the Great Lakes, the depletion of nutrients from the soil were some of the underlying phenomena of "the metabolic rift" in his day. The concept from *Capital* of "the organic composition of capital" expresses in terms of economic quantities this rupture or rift.

Looking back to 1875 we see hints of nature becoming self-conscious, as Elisée Reclus put it. About the time Marx was composing this critique, the first Arbor Day (April 22, 1872) celebrated by planting trees was announced in the USA, and John Muir was walking in the Rockies and asking, "How Shall We Preserve Our Forests?" While these were only "flea-hops" as Marx might say (see below), they were signs of what lay ahead.

Nature is the beginning both of life and of capitalism. "The bourgeois have very good grounds for falsely ascribing *supernatural creative power* to labor, since it follows precisely from labor's dependance on nature that workers with no other property than their labor power must, in all conditions of society and culture, be the slave of other human beings who have made themselves the owners of the material conditions of labor. He can only work by their permission and hence only live with their permission." In *Capital* this will be called expropriation and exploitation. In the young Marx it will be called alienation. Marx lifts the veil. To our world, to nature, to the biosphere, to creation, to the commons. Only the working class, he writes in the Gotha critique, can "lift this historical curse."

Between the two critiques, 1844–75, lay thirty years of class struggle, revolution, war, empire, and massive constructions of iron and steel, and Marx indeed threw away the imaginary flower to pluck the living flower. After the failures of the revolutions of 1848 he turned his attention to the demolition of the bourgeois divisions of politics from economics in perhaps the greatest critique ever made in the *Grundrisse* (1857) and *Capital* (1867). These outlined the "wicked *ways*" of capital and established "the truth of this world." They provide the means of plucking the living flower.

Could this critique become the soul, the heart, the sigh of the oppressed? It is no longer a philosophical or spiritual question; it is a political question.

One of his principal forms of critique is to describe the arguments of his opponent as "words" or "phrases" denying to them any substance in reason or factual evidence. He does this repeatedly in the *Critique of the Gotha Program*: a sentence "limps," "hollow phrases," "bungled in style," "mere phrases," "obsolete verbal rubbish," "false Lassallean formulation," "a newspaper scribbler's phrase." Yet the critique contains two signature phrases of the Marxist outlook. One of them is both a profound summary of the fundamental opposition to capitalism and a fighting slogan for the banners of revolution, "From each according to their abilities, to each according to their needs."[4] This is the seed of the living flower.

The apostle Luke describes these early Christians who "had all things common" (Acts 4:32) "and distribution was made unto every man according as he had need" (Acts 4:35). When threatened with famine during the reign of Claudius, relief was obtained from "every man according to his ability" (Acts 11:29).

What is it that abilities are creating? What is it that needs are accepting? Are we to interpret these two processes as production and consumption? In capitalist society production and consumption form a whole, the economy, regulated by the market, whose unit is the commodity, and whose lingo is money. This is the "historical curse."

If you think about it, there seems to be some mysterious agent who measures out those abilities (senior management? HR?) or who doles out according to needs (Amazon? retail?). It is this mystery which can only be described in the future, "after the revolution." Is it traditional institutions of civil society—family, work, government? Is it revolutionary assemblies—the congregation, the city square, the soviet, some new version of the tribe? Is it some other social organization? Elinor Ostrom formulated it as "the governance of the commons."[5] Marx relies neither on Providence nor on Progress for the realization of the future. The mystical former relies on divine agency and the abstract latter depends on Victorian technological and utilitarian belief. It does not happen automatically or inevitably. Earlier in the *Grundrisse* he had written "of the rich individuality which is as all-sided in its production as in its consumption, and whose labour also therefore appears no longer as labour, but as the full development of activity itself."[6]

He refers to the "the common satisfaction of needs such as schools, health services, etc." He refers to "the common stock." The French revolutionary socialist Jean Jaurès said, "Just as all citizens exercise political power in a democratic manner in common, so they must exercise economic power in common as well."[7] Communist society, Marx writes, "*emerges* from capitalist society which is thus in every respect economically, morally, and intellectually, still stamped with the birthmarks of the old society from whose womb it emerges."

What is the relationship between the statement of principles and the enumerated points of the program? In *The Communist Manifesto* (1848) the relationship was mediated by the history of class struggle. In the *Critique of the Gotha Program* the relationship depends on that critique of political economy found in *Capital* (1867) and the *Grundrisse* (1857).

In analyzing Marx's thought we remind ourselves that thought is in motion. His ideas at any one time are not fixed in an eternity of truth. On the contrary they are very much of his times. So in understanding the problems of 1875 in the Gotha Program, we can both think back to earlier phases of his thinking and forward to their subsequent development. We go back to the "young Marx" and forward to the "old Marx."[8]

The "young Marx" is all about alienation; he gives us both a spiritual and philosophical lens. The "old Marx" is all about the commons; he gives us a lens in revolutionary anthropology and immersion in the so-called backward countries where indeed the air is better. Together the ideas of the young and the old Marx provide us with a way to read the *Critique of the Gotha Program*. We are no longer confined to the realm of political economy.

We can approach both the meaning of communism and the anticapitalist transition to it in ways that may be helpful in the twenty-first century.

The "mature Marx" remains central, which is to say that the critical analysis of the capitalist mode of production and the critique of political economy are what he is all about as he disentangles the hopeless web of error and bad politics found in the Gotha Program. Its guiding author, Ferdinand Lassalle, was formerly a follower of Marx who later allied with the Junkers, the German landlord class. Yet the lords of the land turned nature into a commodity, a means of constant capital, and thus an instrument of extraction and exploitation. Such are the wicked ways.

The preface (1867) to *Das Kapital* Volume I boldly proclaims, "Just as in the eighteenth century the American War of Independence sounded the tocsin for the European middle class, so in the nineteenth century the American Civil War did the same for the European working class."[9] The Civil War sounded the death knell of slavery with the horn of the jubilee. That tocsin will ring to the European working class with the Paris Commune of 1871 and reverberate with the working classes of the world ongoing.

In the Paris Commune, during the seventy-two days of its life, the abolition of the death penalty and the burning of the guillotine, the destruction of the Vendôme column to the Napoleonic empire, and the formation of the Women's Union provided an idea of working-class self-government, or the political imaginary of *commune*.[10] Said Marx, "The great social measure of the Commune was its own working existence."[11] As a result of the Commune Marx revised *The Communist Manifesto* to include the sentence, "the working class cannot simply lay hold of the ready-made state machinery and wield it for their own purpose."

In the summer of 1871 Peter Kropotkin ("mutual aid") was in Finland, William Morris ("fellowship") was in Iceland, and Karl Marx in London was studying the Russian language and reading Chernyshevsky's *Essays on the Communal Ownership of*

Land. His guide was the young Russian exile and Communard Elisabeth Dmitrieff, who besides leading Marx to the study of the peasant commune in Russia (the *obshchina)*, was also the organizer of the seamstresses, laundresses, and dressmakers of Paris into the Women's Union for the Defense of Paris and Aid to the Wounded. In Geneva discussions took place among veterans and exiles during the 1870s that produced the idea of "anarchist communism," or the dissolution of State, Nation, and Capital.

The Commune was at the center of worldwide revolt. The writing of the *Critique of the Gotha Program* coincided with the hanging of nineteen coal miners (the "Molly Maguires"), with the police riot at Tompkins Square in New York, with the internment of the Navajo nation, the expropriation of the Comanches, the cultural war ("kill the Indian, save the man"), Geronimo ("I was born where there were no enclosures") escaping the San Carlos Reservation, and the African American military mobilization as "buffalo soldiers" to annihilate the bison that had provided subsistence for the indigenous people of the plains. Thus did capital create and then use our divisions. The path was cleared for the global seizures and massacres in Africa, Asia, and Wounded Knee.[12]

The Kabylie revolt in Algeria against French conquest and confiscation of the common lands occurred at the same time as the Paris Commune. Two hundred fifty tribes rose up, village assemblies providing the base along the coast, up the mountains, to the desert. It was led by Cheikh Mokrani. The infamous Warnier Law of 1873 expropriated communal lands in Algeria, "tearing away the Arabs from their nature bond to the soil."[13] At the end of his life in 1882 Marx spent two months in Algeria hoping that the commons of air in North Africa would heal the damage done to his lungs by capitalist externalities (i.e., London smog). Marx expressed his admiration of the Algerian Muslims for "the absolute equality of their social intercourse."

Likewise, the defeat of the European working class (the two-month Commune concluded with the bloody massacre of twenty to thirty thousand Communards) signaled the advent of Jim Crow, the end of Reconstruction, the KKK, the Colfax massacre, and the betrayal of the Compromise of 1877 following the 1875 Hayes-Tilden presidential election the next year. Virulent counterrevolution and violent suppression of textile workers of the north and railway workers of the west. "A new slavery arose," wrote W.E.B. Du Bois.[14] "The system of wage labor is a system of slavery," wrote Marx in his *Critique*.

In a letter to Bebel in March 1875 Engels proposed replacing "state" everywhere by *"Gemeinwesen,* a good old German word which can very well convey the meaning of the French word *commune."* The Paris Commune four years earlier was, Marx said, "the glorious harbinger of a new society." The mixture of commune, commons, and communism was a heady semantic mix concealing a revolutionary riddle not yet solved.

> The question then arises: What transformation will the body politic undergo in communist society? In other words what social functions analogous to present state functions will remain at that juncture. This question can only be answered scientifically, and one does not get a flea-hop nearer to the problem by a thousandfold combination of the word "people" with the word "state" [as Lassalle did in the Gotha program].
>
> Between capitalist and communist society there lies the period of the revolutionary transformation of the one into the other. Corresponding to this is also a political transition period in which the state can be nothing but *the revolutionary dictatorship of the proletariat.*

We can say that this is, at least, a flea-hop.

The second key phrase in the *Critique of the Gotha Program* is "the dictatorship of the proletariat." In 2020 Mike Stout, the Pittsburgh steelworker and singer-songwriter, gave one explanation: "The only 'dictatorship' I envision is one that doesn't let the greedy 1% and their class drive us into indebted servitude, while squandering and hoarding our wealth and natural resources, and stops them from destroying the whole planet."[15] Engels gave a similar explanation. In the same year that he published Marx's *Critique of the Gotha Program* (1891), he asked, "Do you want to know what the dictatorship of the proletariat looks like?" and answered, "Look at the Paris Commune. That was the dictatorship of the proletariat."

Marx had used the phrase once before in a letter (March 5, 1852) to Joseph Weydemeyer (1818–66). "My own contribution," wrote Marx, "was (1) to show that the existence of classes is merely bound up with certain historical phases in the development of production; (2) that the class struggle necessarily leads to the dictatorship of the proletariat; [and] (3) that this dictatorship, itself, constitutes no more than a transition to the abolition of all classes and to a classless society."[16]

Weydemeyer went to America and became a lieutenant colonel in the Union Army. He surveyed Central Park, and he designed the defenses of St. Louis while distributing copies of Marx's Inaugural Address to the International. Marx's address addressed the ditch diggers and hod carriers of these earthen works, pointing to the day "like slave labour, like serf labour, hired labour is but a transitory and inferior form, destined to disappear before associated labour plying its toil with a willing hand, a ready mind, and a joyous heart"![17]

"To conquer political power has therefore become the great duty of the working classes," he wrote just as Black Reconstruction was beginning. Success depended not on numbers alone but upon knowledge particularly of solidarity, and that led to the formation in 1864 of the International. Emancipation of the working classes entailed "the abolition of all class rule."[18]

We are familiar with the dictatorship of the bourgeoisie: the democratic Levellers of the 1640s were followed by the dictator Cromwell, the insurgent Jacobins of the 1790s were followed by the emperor Napoleon, the Russian Bolsheviks of the 1920s were followed by Stalin. Marx had learned from the Paris Commune that the proletariat cannot simply take over the state and use it for its own purposes. It must smash the state.

W.E.B. Du Bois intended to call his chapter on Black Reconstruction in South Carolina "The Dictatorship of the Black Proletariat in South Carolina" but changed it simply to

"The Black Proletariat in South Carolina." He made this change after it was brought to his attention that "universal suffrage does not lead to a real dictatorship until workers use their votes consciously to rid themselves of the dominion of private capital." He adds, "There were signs of such an object among South Carolina Negroes, but it was always coupled with the idea of that day, that the only real escape for a laborer was himself to own capital." Dictatorship is a "stopgap pending the work of universal education, equitable income, and strong character."[19] He writes of the "dictatorship of capital" in the North, a plutocracy. When Du Bois chose not to use the phrase "dictatorship of the proletariat" it was because the suffrage was used to promote *individual* rather than *collective* ownership.

We now write "history from below." The expression includes histories of the oppressed, whether that is labor history or women's history or indigenous people's history or African American history or even (to use an old term) natural history. In every example the "below" implies an "above." It implies a contrast or an unspoken opposite, namely ruling-class history, which is reified as economic history, then history of the state, then history of war. These are aspects of what the Zapatistas call the war of oblivion. Indeed, deliberate forgetting is one of capital's wicked ways.

The anarchist Mikhail Bakunin asked, "Will perhaps the proletariat as a whole head the government?" Marx answers, "There will in fact be no below then." History from below comes to an end just as class rule comes to an end.[20] Class rule over the resisting strata continues "until the economic basis that makes the existence of classes possible has been destroyed."

The view that Marx and Engels "rigidly refused to paint pictures of the future communist society," as Eric Hobsbawm says, is only a half-truth. Marx did not paint pictures with brush and oil; he took photographs. That is to say, he sought the commune in the *real* movement. This is the significance of Chernyshevsky, of Henry Lewis Morgan, of his stay in Algeria, of his letters to Zasulich. Hobsbawm says that Marx was provoked "into a theoretical statement which, if probably not new, had at any rate not been publicly formulated by him before."[21] It wasn't a question of "new" or not. To Marx theory generated the project of revolutionary investigation.

The Ethnological Notebooks are one of the major works of the "late Marx." They contain, among other things, close study from Lewis Henry Morgan of the five nations of the Iroquois, or the Haudenosaunee. The *Notebooks* delighted the Chicago surrealist Franklin Rosemont, who took joy in Marx's multiple references by the Iroquois and Muscokees to the species of "Turtle Island"—elk, raccoon, buffalo, turtle, eagle, wolf. Marx insists on the importance of imagination to the elevation of human beings. It and the poetic spirit, the spiritual as such, lead us to the real movement.

Marx took note of the Iroquois, whose "democratic assembly where every adult male and female member had a voice upon all questions brought before it." "The women were the great power among the clans," he copied into his notebook.[22] The same text inspired Engels to refer in *The Origin of the Family* to "the world-historic defeat of the female sex."

In February 1881 Vera Zasulich initiated a correspondence with Marx on whether the rural commune, the *obshchina,* could "develop in a socialist direction or whether it was destined to perish as an archaism. Marx wrote several draft replies including a lengthy consideration of common property in history, as a constitutive form (assembly, kinship, clan), and in various ecologies of forest, pasture, meadow. He concluded "that the commune is the fulcrum for social regeneration in Russia."[23]

"The rebuilding, whether it comes now or a century later, will and must go back to the basic principles of Reconstruction in the United States during 1867–1876—Land, Light, and Leading for slaves black, brown, yellow and white, under a dictatorship of the proletariat."[24] It is not quite synonymous with "proletarian hegemony." The values of the material institutions of society have to change to become the ground of government. Hence, the decisive importance of the northern "schoolmarms" or the women who went south during Reconstruction to arm former slaves with the tools of reading, writing, and criticism.

Marx did not publish his *Critique of the Gotha Program*. But five years after he wrote it, the French socialist Jules Guesde visited him in London in May 1880 and asked him to write the preamble to the program of the French Parti Ouvrier or Workers' Party. Marx did so in a dense sentence with many thoughts: the productive class will emancipate all human beings without distinction of sex or race. They can be free only by possessing the means of production collectively. This must be accomplished by revolutionary action which may include universal suffrage as an instrument of emancipation rather than deception. The aim is "the political and economic expropriation of the capitalist class and the return to community of all the means of production."

Here is the commons, here are democracy and universal suffrage, here the phrase "return to the community" implies something lost or expropriated. The term community refers to the collective, cooperative social forms which Marx was studying at the time (the Iroquois, the *obshchina*, Algeria) or what we might call the commons. It is not the state, the market, or the nation. The door is always open for the *"real* movement."

Labor is organized by capital to work. When labor, employed or unemployed, organizes for itself it becomes a class and thus able to save its soul. So the four structures of capitalism and their wicked ways—white supremacy, patriarchy, settler colonialism, and privatization—have caused risings among black and brown people, women, indigenous peoples, and the rebels against extinctions. The immanent possibility arises of these insurgencies becoming components of "the *real* movement which abolishes the present state of things." This is not just an electoral or economic process. We can pluck the living flower to re-create the commons.

Peter Linebaugh
Ann Arbor, Turtle Island

Notes
1   I thank Wendy Goldman, Geoff Eley, and John Garvey for help with bibliography, Riley Linebaugh for suggestions, and Monty Neill for editing.

2   Karl Marx and Frederick Engels, *The German Ideology* (London: Lawrence and Wishart, 1965), 48.

3   Joel Kovel, *The Enemy of Nature: The End of Capitalism or the End of the World* (London: Zed, 2002); John Bellamy Foster, *Marx's Ecology: Materialism and Nature* (New York: Monthly Review Press, 2000); Joel Kovel and Michael Löwy, "An Ecosocialist Manifesto," *Capitalism Nature Socialism*, 2001, https://www.cnsjournal.org/about/an-ecosocialist-manifesto.

4   The phrase is not original to Marx. Louis Blanc had employed it in the 1848 Revolution, it was the epigraph to Saint-Simon's journal, *L'Organisateur*, and Étienne Cabet used it in his utopian fiction, *Voyage en Icarie* (1845).

5   Elinor Ostrom, *Governing the Commons: The Evolution of Institutions for Collective Action* (London: Cambridge University Press, 1990).

6   *Grundrisse*, trans. Martin Nicolaus (New York: Vintage, 1973), 162.

7   Quoted by Geoff Eley, *Forging Democracy: The History of the Left in Europe, 1850–2000* (Oxford: Oxford University Press, 2002), 21.

8   E.P. Thompson notes that Marx, "in his increasing preoccupation in his last years with anthropology, was resuming the projects of his Paris youth." *The Poverty of Theory and Other Essays* (London: Merlin, 1978), 163.

9   *Capital*, trans. Ben Fowkes (London: Penguin, 1976), 91.

10 Kristin Ross, *Communal Luxury: The Political Imaginary of the Paris Commune* (London: Verso, 2015).

11 Karl Marx, *The Civil War in France* (1871).

12 Howard Zinn, *A People's History of the United States* (New York: Harper, 1980), and Roxanne Dunbar-Ortiz, *An Indigenous Peoples' History of the United States* (Boston: Beacon Press, 2014).

13 John Bellamy Foster, Brett Clark, and Hannah Holleman, "Marx and the Indigenous," *Monthly Review* 71, no. 9 (February 2020): 1–19.

14 W.E.B. Du Bois, *Black Reconstruction in America 1860–1880* (New York: Free Press, 1998[1935]), 30.

15 Mike Stout, *Homestead Steel Mill—The Final Ten Years: USWA Local 1397 and the Fight for Union Democracy* (Oakland: PM Press, 2020), 8.

16 *Marx-Engels Collected Works (MECW)*, 39:62–63.

17 *MECW*, 21:330–31.

18 Karl Marx, *The First International and After: Political Writings*, vol. 3, ed. David Fernbach (London: Penguin, 1974), 73–84.

19 Du Bois, *Black Reconstruction*, 381–82.

20 Karl Marx, "The Conspectus of Bakunin's Book *State and Anarchy*," in Karl Marx, Friedrich Engels, and V.I. Lenin, *Anarchism and Anarcho-Syndicalism* (Moscow: Progress Publishers, 1972), 147–52.

21 E.J. Hobsbawm, *How to Change the World: Reflections on Marx and Marxism* (New Haven, CT: Yale University Press, 2011), 47 and 58.

22 Composed in 1880–1882 and published in English for the first time in 1974, see Lawrence Krader, ed., *The Ethnological Notebooks of Karl Marx* (Assen, Netherlands: Van Gorcum, 1974). Franklin Rosemont, "Karl Marx & the Iroquois," *Arsenal: Surrealist Subversion* no. 4 (Chicago: Black Swan Press, 1989), and republished by the Red Balloon Collective as a pamphlet in the Environmental Action Series (ca. 1992).

23 Teodor Shanin, *Late Marx and the Russian Road: Marx and the Peripheries of Capitalism* (London: Routledge, 1983).

24 Du Bois, *Black Reconstruction in America*, 635.

Index

"Passim" (literally "scattered") indicates intermittent discussion of a topic over a cluster of pages.

abstract labor, 7, 9, 10, 13, 32, 35–36n5, 39n36
Algeria: Kabylie revolt, 86
Allgemeiner Deutscher Arbeiterverein (ADAV), 3–4, 11, 12
anthropology, 84, 90
Appel, Jan, 25
automation. See mechanization and automation

Bakunin, Mikhail, 47, 74n7, 89
Bebel, August, 4, 12, 38n23, 74n5
Bible, 79, 83
Bismarck, Otto von, 62, 63
body politic (Staatswesen), 12, 68, 69, 77n39
bourgeoisie, 61, 62, 82, 85; rights, 58
Bracke, Wilhelm, 74n5; Marx letter to, 47–49
Britain, 70, 77n44
Buchez, Philippe, 66, 76n38

Cao, Tian Yu, 29
Capital (Marx), 6, 8, 19, 31, 35–36n5, 40n38, 75n15, 82, 84; first US translations, 21; French edition, 48; preface, 85
Chávez, Hugo, 34
child labor, 72–73

collectivization, 25, 38n22
commodity exchange, 13, 28, 58
commodity production. See production: of commodities
commons, 81–87 passim, 91
communes, 38n22, 87, 89; Russia, 86, 90. See also Paris Commune
communism-socialism distinction and nondistinction. See socialism-communism distinction and nondistinction
Communist International. See Third International
The Communist Manifesto (Marx and Engels), 36n13, 61–62, 84, 85
The Condition of the Working Class in England (Engels), 79, 80
consumption, 9, 55–60 passim, 83, 84; proportion with production, 18, 24
A Contribution to the Critique of Hegel's Philosophy of Right (Marx), 80
cooperative social forms and societies, 2, 14, 67, 91; in Gotha Program, 43, 44, 54–60 passim, 66, 67

"dictatorship of the proletariat," 32–33, 69, 87–89, 90

distribution, 13, 30; in early
    Christianity, 83; in Gotha
    Program, 43, 54–60 passim;
    labor time and, 16, 28, 30. See
    also "from each according to
    his abilities"; redistribution
Dmitrieff, Elisabeth, 86
Du Bois, W.E.B., 87, 88–89
Dunayevskaya, Raya, 2, 15–16,
    24–26 passim

"each according to his abilities."
    See "from each according to his
    abilities"
Economic Problems of Socialism
    (Stalin), 38n22
education, formal, 70–71
Eisenachers. See
    Sozialdemokratische
    Arbeiterpartei Deutschlands
    (SDAP)
Endnotes, 28
Engels, Friedrich, 20, 26, 36n13,
    38n23, 80–81, 87–88; Communist
    Manifesto, 36n13, 61–62, 84, 85;
    Condition of the Working Class,
    79, 80; Origin of the Family, 90
Erfurt Program, 20–21, 26
Ezekiel (New Testament), 79

First International, 12, 35n3, 81;
    formation, 88; Marx address to,
    88; Rules, 54, 60, 62, 75n18
France, 66, 69, 76n25, 77n42, 86, 91.
    See also Paris Commune
freedom, 20, 28, 67, 72
"from each according to his
    abilities," 15–16, 18, 27, 83
Fundamental Principles of
    Communist Production and
    Distribution (Appel), 25

Gotha Program, 3, 6, 9–12 passim,
    27; Critique, 51–74; text, 43–45
Great Britain. See Britain
Grundrisse (Marx), 29, 40n38, 82, 84
Guesde, Jules, 91

Haudenosaunee Confederacy. See
    Iroquois Confederacy
Hobsbawm, Eric, 89–90

Indigenous Americans. See Native
    Americans
"instruments of labor"
    (Arbeitsmittel), 51, 75n15
internationalism, 63. See also
    First International; Second
    International; Third
    International
International Workingmen's
    Association. See First
    International
Iroquois Confederacy, 90

Jaurès, Jean, 84

Kautsky, Karl, 20, 26

labor productivity. See
    productivity
labor time, 13–18 passim, 23–31
    passim, 39n33. See also socially
    necessary labor time; workday
labor unions. See unions
Lange, Friedrich Albert, 64, 76n36
Lange, Oskar, 38n27
Lassalle, Ferdinand, 1–9 passim,
    20–23 passim, 36n12, 48, 75n10;
    "iron law of wages," 11, 20,
    63–64; Marx on, 54–55, 56, 61–66
    passim
Lebowitz, Michael, 33–34
Lenin, Vladimir, 12, 21–24 passim;
    State and Revolution, 22, 23
Liebknecht, Wilhelm, 4, 12, 22,
    38n23, 47, 74n5
Liverpool Financial Reform
    Association, 70, 77n44
lower middle class, 61
Lueer, Hermann, 34
Luxemburg, Rosa, 21, 36n12

Malthus, Thomas, 11, 76n36
Mao Zedong, 38n22

Marx, Jenny, 38n23
Marx, Karl: *Communist Manifesto*, 36n13, 61–62, 84, 85; *Contribution to the Critique of Hegel's Philosophy of Right*, 80; *Grundrisse*, 29, 40n38, 82, 84. See also *Capital* (Marx)
Marxist-Humanists, 2, 27
mechanization and automation, 29–30, 37n20, 75n15
middle class. *See* bourgeoisie; lower middle class
Mokrani Revolt. See Algeria: Kabylie revolt

nationalism, 11, 12
nationalization, 8, 20, 24
Native Americans, 86, 90
nature, 10, 51, 81–82

The Origin of the Family (Engels), 90
Ostrom, Elinor, 83

Paris Commune, 5, 81, 85–86, 87, 88
Parti Ouvrier, 91
Postone, Moishe, 39n36
private ownership, 8, 25, 53; of labor power, 34
production, 25, 37n16, 57, 60, 65, 84, 85; collective / cooperative, 2; of commodities, 9, 17; proportion with consumption, 18, 24
productivity, 6–7, 29, 59, 65
proletariat (working classes), 4, 61, 63, 81, 88, 89. See also *The Condition of the Working Class* (Engels); "dictatorship of the proletariat"
property, private ownership of. *See* private ownership

quid pro quo, 17, 18, 27

redistribution, 10–11; Venezuela, 34
religion, 72, 80. *See also* Bible

rights, 58–59
Rousseau, Jean-Jacques, 52, 75n16
Russia, 67; February Revolution, 22; *obshchina*, 86, 90; October (Bolshevik) Revolution, 23–24

SAPD. *See* Sozialistische Arbeiterpartei Deutschlands (SAPD)
schooling. *See* education, formal
SDAP. *See* Sozialdemokratische Arbeiterpartei Deutschlands (SDAP)
SDP. *See* Sozialdemokratische Partei Deutschlands (SPD)
Second International, 21, 22, 23, 74n5
Sève, Lucien, 12
socialism-communism distinction and nondistinction, 12, 19–20, 36n13
socially necessary labor time, 6, 7, 9, 13–19 passim, 26, 30
Sozialdemokratische Arbeiterpartei Deutschlands (SDAP), 1, 4, 11, 12, 35n3, 38n23, 74n5
Sozialdemokratische Partei Deutschlands (SPD), 20, 21
Sozialistische Arbeiterpartei Deutschlands (SAPD), 4, 6, 20; Erfurt Program, 20–21, 26. *See also* Gotha Program
Staatswesen. See body politic (*Staatswesen*)
Stalin, Joseph, 24, 29, 38n27, 88; *Economic Problems of Socialism*, 38n22
Stalinism, 2, 11, 25, 26, 29
The State and Revolution (Lenin), 22, 23
state-capitalism, 24, 25
Stout, Mike, 87
surplus value, 10, 11, 31, 65
Switzerland, 69, 70

Third International, 23

trade unions. *See* unions

unions, 11, 35n3, 36n12
United States, 86, 88; Civil War,
    85, 88; formal education, 71;
    Marx on, 85; Reconstruction,
    88–89, 90
"useful labor," 43, 51, 52–53
use value, 7, 10, 13, 17, 29, 30, 36n7;
    in Gotha Program, 51, 53

value, 6–11 passim, 13, 24, 26, 29.
    See also surplus value; use value
vanguard party, 21–22, 23
Venezuela, 34–35

wage labor, 18, 23, 65, 87; abolition
    of, 15, 64
wages, 17, 63–65 passim; "iron law
    of," 11, 20, 63–64
women's labor, 72; unions, 86
workday, 72
working classes. *See* proletariat
    (working classes)
working time. *See* labor time

Zasulich, Vera, 90

About the Contributors

Karl Marx was a German philosopher, economist, historian, sociologist, political theorist, journalist, and socialist revolutionary, and the author of *The Communist Manifesto* and *Capital: A Critique of Political Economy*.

Kevin B. Anderson is professor of sociology at University of California, Santa Barbara, with appointments in feminist studies and political science. He is the author of *Lenin, Hegel, and Western Marxism*; *Foucault and the Iranian Revolution* (with Janet Afary); and *Marx at the Margins*.

Karel Ludenhoff is an Amsterdam-based labor activist and a writer on Marx's critique of political economy whose essays have appeared in *Logos* and other journals.

Peter Hudis is professor of philosophy and humanities at Oakton College and author of *Marx's Concept of the Alternative to Capitalism* and *Frantz Fanon: Philosopher of the Barricades*. He edited *The Rosa Luxemburg Reader* and *The Letters of Rosa Luxemburg*.

Peter Linebaugh is the author of *The London Hanged*; *The Many-Headed Hydra* (with Marcus Rediker); *The Magna Carta Manifesto*; *Stop, Thief!*; and *The Incomplete, True, Authentic, and Wonderful History of May Day*. He has also contributed introductions to Verso's selection of Thomas Paine's writings and the PM Press edition of E.P. Thompson's *William Morris: Romantic to Revolutionary*. He lives in the region of the Great Lakes and retired from the University of Toledo in Ohio in 2014.

ABOUT PM PRESS

PM Press is an independent, radical publisher of books and media to educate, entertain, and inspire. Founded in 2007 by a small group of people with decades of publishing, media, and organizing experience, PM Press amplifies the voices of radical authors, artists, and activists. Our aim is to deliver bold political ideas and vital stories to all walks of life and arm the dreamers to demand the impossible. We have sold millions of copies of our books, most often one at a time, face to face. We're old enough to know what we're doing and young enough to know what's at stake. Join us to create a better world.

PM Press
PO Box 23912
Oakland, CA 94623
www.pmpress.org

PM Press in Europe
europe@pmpress.org
www.pmpress.org.uk

FRIENDS OF PM PRESS

These are indisputably momentous times—the financial system is melting down globally and the Empire is stumbling. Now more than ever there is a vital need for radical ideas.

In the many years since its founding—and on a mere shoestring—PM Press has risen to the formidable challenge of publishing and distributing knowledge and entertainment for the struggles ahead. With hundreds of releases to date, we have published an impressive and stimulating array of literature, art, music, politics, and culture. Using every available medium, we've succeeded in connecting those hungry for ideas and information to those putting them into practice.

Friends of PM allows you to directly help impact, amplify, and revitalize the discourse and actions of radical writers, filmmakers, and artists. It provides us with a stable foundation from which we can build upon our early successes and provides a much-needed subsidy for the materials that can't necessarily pay their own way. You can help make that happen—and receive every new title automatically delivered to your door once a month—by joining as a Friend of PM Press. And, we'll throw in a free T-shirt when you sign up.

Here are your options:

- **$30 a month** Get all books and pamphlets plus 50% discount on all webstore purchases

- **$40 a month** Get all PM Press releases (including CDs and DVDs) plus 50% discount on all webstore purchases

- **$100 a month** Superstar—Everything plus PM merchandise, free downloads, and 50% discount on all webstore purchases

For those who can't afford $30 or more a month, we have **Sustainer Rates** at $15, $10 and $5. Sustainers get a free PM Press T-shirt and a 50% discount on all purchases from our website.

Your Visa or Mastercard will be billed once a month, until you tell us to stop. Or until our efforts succeed in bringing the revolution around. Or the financial meltdown of Capital makes plastic redundant. Whichever comes first.

From ▆SPECTRE▶ from PM Press

Stop, Thief!
The Commons, Enclosures,
and Resistance

Peter Linebaugh

ISBN: 978-1-60486-747-3
$21.95   304 pages

In this majestic tour de force, celebrated
historian Peter Linebaugh takes aim at the
thieves of land, the polluters of the seas, the
ravagers of the forests, the despoilers of rivers, and the removers of
mountaintops. Scarcely a society has existed on the face of the earth
that has not had commoning at its heart. "Neither the state nor the
market," say the planetary commoners. These essays kindle the embers
of memory to ignite our future commons.

From Thomas Paine to the Luddites, from Karl Marx—who concluded
his great study of capitalism with the enclosure of commons—to the
practical dreamer William Morris—who made communism into a verb
and advocated communizing industry and agriculture—to the 20th-
century communist historian E.P. Thompson, Linebaugh brings to life the
vital commonist tradition. He traces the red thread from the great revolt
of commoners in 1381 to the enclosures of Ireland, and the American
commons, where European immigrants who had been expelled from
their commons met the immense commons of the native peoples
and the underground African-American urban commons. Illuminating
these struggles in this indispensable collection, Linebaugh reignites the
ancient cry, "STOP, THIEF!"

"There is not a more important historian living today. Period."
—Robin D.G. Kelley, author of *Freedom Dreams: The Black Radical
Imagination*

*"E.P. Thompson, you may rest now. Linebaugh restores the dignity of
the despised luddites with a poetic grace worthy of the master . . .
[A] commonist manifesto for the 21st century."*
—Mike Davis, author of *Planet of Slums*

*"Peter Linebaugh's great act of historical imagination . . . takes the cliché
of 'globalization' and makes it live. The local and the global are once again
shown to be inseparable—as they are, at present, for the machine-breakers
of the new world crisis."*
—T.J. Clark, author of *Farewell to an Idea*

From ■SPECTRE▶ from PM Press

The Incomplete, True, Authentic, and Wonderful History of May Day

Peter Linebaugh

ISBN: 978-1-62963-107-3
$15.95   200 pages

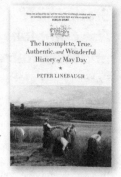

"May Day is about affirmation, the love of life, and the start of spring, so it has to be about the beginning of the end of the capitalist system of exploitation, oppression, war, and overall misery, toil, and moil." So writes celebrated historian Peter Linebaugh in an essential compendium of reflections on the reviled, glorious, and voltaic occasion of May 1st.

It is a day that has made the rich and powerful cower in fear and caused Parliament to ban the Maypole—a magnificent and riotous day of rebirth, renewal, and refusal. These reflections on the Red and the Green—out of which arguably the only hope for the future lies—are populated by the likes of Native American anarcho-communist Lucy Parsons, the Dodge Revolutionary Union Movement, Karl Marx, José Martí, W.E.B. Du Bois, Rosa Luxemburg, SNCC, and countless others, both sentient and verdant. The book is a forceful reminder of the potentialities of the future, for the coming of a time when the powerful will fall, the commons restored, and a better world born anew.

"There is not a more important historian living today. Period."
—Robin D.G. Kelley, author of *Freedom Dreams: The Black Radical Imagination*

"E.P. Thompson, you may rest now. Linebaugh restores the dignity of the despised luddites with a poetic grace worthy of the master."
—Mike Davis, author of *Planet of Slums*

"Ideas can be beautiful too, and the ideas Peter Linebaugh provokes and maps in this history of liberty are dazzling reminders of what we have been and who we could be."
—Rebecca Solnit, author of *Storming the Gates of Paradise*

From SPECTRE from PM Press
CLASSICS

William Morris: Romantic to Revolutionary

E.P. Thompson

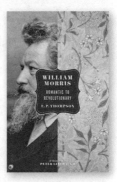

ISBN: 978-1-60486-243-0
$32.95   880 pages

William Morris—the great 19th-century craftsman, architect, designer, poet and writer—remains a monumental figure whose influence resonates powerfully today. As an intellectual (and author of the seminal utopian *News from Nowhere*), his concern with artistic and human values led him to cross what he called the "river of fire" and become a committed socialist—committed not to some theoretical formula but to the day-by-day struggle of working women and men in Britain and to the evolution of his ideas about art, about work and about how life should be lived. Many of his ideas accorded none too well with the reforming tendencies dominant in the labour movement, nor with those of "orthodox" Marxism, which has looked elsewhere for inspiration. Both sides have been inclined to venerate Morris rather than to pay attention to what he said. Originally written less than a decade before his groundbreaking *The Making of the English Working Class*, E.P. Thompson brought to this biography his now trademark historical mastery, passion, wit, and essential sympathy. It remains unsurpassed as the definitive work on this remarkable figure, by the major British historian of the 20th century.

"Two impressive figures, William Morris as subject and E.P. Thompson as author, are conjoined in this immense biographical-historical-critical study, and both of them have gained in stature since the first edition of the book was published . . . The book that was ignored in 1955 has meanwhile become something of an underground classic—almost impossible to locate in second-hand bookstores, pored over in libraries, required reading for anyone interested in Morris and, increasingly, for anyone interested in one of the most important of contemporary British historians . . . Thompson has the distinguishing characteristic of a great historian: he has transformed the nature of the past, it will never look the same again; and whoever works in the area of his concerns in the future must come to terms with what Thompson has written. So too with his study of William Morris."
—Peter Stansky, *The New York Times Book Review*

"An absorbing biographical study . . . A glittering quarry of marvelous quotes from Morris and others, many taken from heretofore inaccessible or unpublished sources."
—Walter Arnold, *Saturday Review*

From **SPECTRE** from PM Press

Patriarchy of the Wage: Notes on Marx, Gender, and Feminism

Silvia Federici

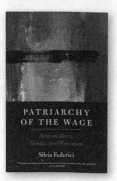

ISBN: 978-1-62963-799-0
$15.00   152 pages

At a time when socialism is entering a historic crisis and we are witnessing a worldwide expansion of capitalist relations, a feminist rethinking of Marx's work is vitally important. In *Patriarchy of the Wage*, Silvia Federici, best-selling author and the most important Marxist feminist of our time, asks why Marx and the Marxist tradition were so crucial in their denunciation of capitalism's exploitation of human labor and blind to women's work and struggle on the terrain of social reproduction. Why was Marx unable to anticipate the profound transformations in the proletarian family that took place at the turn of the nineteenth century creating a new patriarchal regime?

In this fiery collection of penetrating essays published here for the first time, Federici carefully examines these questions and in the process has provided an expansive redefinition of work, class, and class-gender relations. Seeking to delineate the specific character of capitalist "patriarchalism," this magnificently original approach also highlights Marx's and the Marxist tradition's problematic view of industrial production and the State in the struggle for human liberation. Federici's lucid argument that most reproductive work is irreducible to automation is a powerful reminder of the poverty of the revolutionary imagination that consigns to the world of machines the creation of the material conditions for a communist society.

Patriarchy of the Wage does more than just redefine classical Marxism; it is an explosive call for a new kind of communism. Read this book and realize the power and importance of reproductive labor!

"Silvia Federici's work embodies an energy that urges us to rejuvenate struggles against all types of exploitation and, precisely for that reason, her work produces a common: a common sense of the dissidence that creates a community in struggle."
—Maria Mies, coauthor of *Ecofeminism*

"Federici has become a crucial figure for young Marxists, political theorists, and a new generation of feminists."
—Rachel Kushner author of *The Flamethrowers*

Re-enchanting the World: Feminism and the Politics of the Commons

Silvia Federici
with a Foreword by Peter Linebaugh

ISBN: 978-1-62963-569-9
$19.95   240 pages

Silvia Federici is one of the most important
contemporary theorists of capitalism and
feminist movements. In this collection of her work spanning over twenty
years, she provides a detailed history and critique of the politics of the
commons from a feminist perspective. In her clear and combative voice,
Federici provides readers with an analysis of some of the key issues and
debates in contemporary thinking on this subject.

Drawing on rich historical research, she maps the connections
between the previous forms of enclosure that occurred with the
birth of capitalism and the destruction of the commons and the "new
enclosures" at the heart of the present phase of global capitalist
accumulation. Considering the commons from a feminist perspective,
this collection centers on women and reproductive work as crucial to
both our economic survival and the construction of a world free from
the hierarchies and divisions capital has planted in the body of the world
proletariat. Federici is clear that the commons should not be understood
as happy islands in a sea of exploitative relations but rather autonomous
spaces from which to challenge the existing capitalist organization of life
and labor.

*"Silvia Federici's theoretical capacity to articulate the plurality that fuels the
contemporary movement of women in struggle provides a true toolbox for
building bridges between different features and different people."*
—Massimo De Angelis, professor of political economy, University of
East London

*"Silvia Federici's work embodies an energy that urges us to rejuvenate
struggles against all types of exploitation and, precisely for that reason, her
work produces a common: a common sense of the dissidence that creates a
community in struggle."*
—Maria Mies, coauthor of *Ecofeminism*

From SPECTRE from PM Press

Capital and Its Discontents: Conversations with Radical Thinkers in a Time of Tumult

Sasha Lilley

ISBN: 978-1-60486-334-5
$20.00   320 pages

Capitalism is stumbling, empire is faltering, and the planet is thawing. Yet many people are still grasping to understand these multiple crises and to find a way forward to a just future. Into the breach come the essential insights of *Capital and Its Discontents*, which cut through the gristle to get to the heart of the matter about the nature of capitalism and imperialism, capitalism's vulnerabilities at this conjuncture—and what can we do to hasten its demise. Through a series of incisive conversations with some of the most eminent thinkers and political economists on the Left—including David Harvey, Ellen Meiksins Wood, Mike Davis, Leo Panitch, Tariq Ali, and Noam Chomsky—*Capital and Its Discontents* illuminates the dynamic contradictions undergirding capitalism and the potential for its dethroning. At a moment when capitalism as a system is more reviled than ever, here is an indispensable toolbox of ideas for action by some of the most brilliant thinkers of our times.

"These conversations illuminate the current world situation in ways that are very useful for those hoping to orient themselves and find a way forward to effective individual and collective action. Highly recommended."
—Kim Stanley Robinson, *New York Times* bestselling author of the *Mars Trilogy* and *The Years of Rice and Salt*

"In this fine set of interviews, an A-list of radical political economists demonstrate why their skills are indispensable to understanding today's multiple economic and ecological crises."
—Raj Patel, author of *Stuffed and Starved* and *The Value of Nothing*

"This is an extremely important book. It is the most detailed, comprehensive, and best study yet published on the most recent capitalist crisis and its discontents. Sasha Lilley sets each interview in its context, writing with style, scholarship, and wit about ideas and philosophies."
—Andrej Grubačić, radical sociologist and social critic, co-author of *Wobblies and Zapatistas*

Adventure Capitalism: A History of Libertarian Exit, from the Era of Decolonization to the Digital Age

Raymond Craib

ADVENTURE CAPITALISM

"Brilliant... a fascinating story."
—GREG GRANDIN, author of *The End of the Myth*

A History of Libertarian Exit, from the Era of Decolonization to the Digital Age

■SPECTRE▶ RAYMOND B. CRAIB

ISBN: 978-1-62963-917-8
$24.95   304 pages

Imagine a capitalist paradise. An island utopia governed solely by the rules of the market and inspired by the fictions of Ayn Rand and Robinson Crusoe. Sound far-fetched? It may not be. The past half century is littered with the remains of such experiments in what Raymond Craib calls "libertarian exit." Often dismissed as little more than the dreams of crazy, rich Caucasians, exit strategies have been tried out from the southwest Pacific to the Caribbean, from the North Sea to the high seas, often with dire consequences for local inhabitants. Based on research in archives in the US, the UK, and Vanuatu, as well as in FBI files acquired through the Freedom of Information Act, Craib explores in careful detail the ideology and practice of libertarian exit and its place in the histories of contemporary capitalism, decolonization, empire, and oceans and islands. *Adventure Capitalism* is a global history that intersects with an array of figures: Fidel Castro and the Koch brothers, American segregationists and Melanesian socialists, Honolulu-based real estate speculators and British Special Branch spies, soldiers of fortune and English lords, Orange County engineers and Tongan navigators, CIA operatives and CBS news executives, and a new breed of techno-utopians and an old guard of Honduran coup leaders. This is not only a history of our time but, given the new iterations of privatized exit—seasteads, free private cities, and space colonization—it is also a history of our future.

"The libertarian quest for 'land no one is using' inevitably finds 'land that is used by all,' and the ugly conflation of the two sends the champions of personal liberty in search of guns, indentured servants, and death squads."
—Cory Doctorow

From ■SPECTRE▶ from PM Press

Pictures of a Gone City: Tech and the Dark Side of Prosperity in the San Francisco Bay Area

Richard A. Walker

ISBN: 978-1-62963-510-1
$26.95   480 pages

The San Francisco Bay Area is currently the jewel in the crown of capitalism—the tech capital of the world and a gusher of wealth from the Silicon Gold Rush. It has been generating jobs, spawning new innovation, and spreading ideas that are changing lives everywhere. It boasts of being the Left Coast, the Greenest City, and the best place for workers in the USA. So what could be wrong? It may seem that the Bay Area has the best of it in Trump's America, but there is a dark side of success: overheated bubbles and spectacular crashes; exploding inequality and millions of underpaid workers; a boiling housing crisis, mass displacement, and severe environmental damage; a delusional tech elite and complicity with the worst in American politics.

This sweeping account of the Bay Area in the age of the tech boom covers many bases. It begins with the phenomenal concentration of IT in Greater Silicon Valley, the fabulous economic growth of the bay region and the unbelievable wealth piling up for the 1% and high incomes of Upper Classes—in contrast to the fate of the working class and people of color earning poverty wages and struggling to keep their heads above water. The middle chapters survey the urban scene, including the greatest housing bubble in the United States, a metropolis exploding in every direction, and a geography turned inside out. Lastly, it hits the environmental impact of the boom, the fantastical ideology of Tech World, and the political implications of the tech-led transformation of the bay region.

"With Pictures of a Gone City, *California's greatest geographer tells us how the Bay Area has become the global center of hi-tech capitalism. Drawing on a lifetime of research, Richard Walker dismantles the mythology of the New Economy, placing its creativity in a long history of power, work, and struggles for justice.*"
—Jason W. Moore, author of *Capitalism in the Web of Life*

Mutual Aid: An Illuminated Factor of Evolution

Peter Kropotkin
Illustrated by N.O. Bonzo with an
Introduction by David Graeber
& Andrej Grubačić, Foreword by
Ruth Kinna, Postscript by GATS,
and an Afterword by Allan Antliff

ISBN: 978-1-62963-874-4
$20.00   336 pages

One hundred years after his death, Peter Kropotkin is still one of the most inspirational figures of the anarchist movement. It is often forgotten that Kropotkin was also a world-renowned geographer whose seminal critique of the hypothesis of competition promoted by social Darwinism helped revolutionize modern evolutionary theory. An admirer of Darwin, he used his observations of life in Siberia as the basis for his 1902 collection of essays *Mutual Aid: A Factor of Evolution*. Kropotkin demonstrated that mutually beneficial cooperation and reciprocity—in both individuals and as a species—plays a far more important role in the animal kingdom and human societies than does individualized competitive struggle. Kropotkin carefully crafted his theory making the science accessible. His account of nature rejected Rousseau's romantic depictions and ethical socialist ideas that cooperation was motivated by the notion of "universal love." His understanding of the dynamics of social evolution shows us the power of cooperation—whether it is bison defending themselves against a predator or workers unionizing against their boss. His message is clear: solidarity is strength!

Every page of this new edition of *Mutual Aid* has been beautifully illustrated by one of anarchism's most celebrated current artists, N.O. Bonzo. The reader will also enjoy original artwork by GATS and insightful commentary by David Graeber, Ruth Kinna, Andrej Grubačić, and Allan Antliff.

"N.O. Bonzo has created a rare document, updating Kropotkin's anarchist classic Mutual Aid, *by intertwining compelling imagery with an updated text. Filled with illustrious examples, their art gives the words and histories, past and present, resonance for new generations to seed flowers of cooperation to push through the concrete of resistance to show liberatory possibilities for collective futures."*
—scott crow, author of *Black Flags and Windmills* and *Setting Sights*

Anarchy, Geography, Modernity: Selected Writings of Elisée Reclus

Edited by John P. Clark and
Camille Martin

ISBN: 978-1-60486-429-8
$22.95   304 pages

Anarchy, Geography, Modernity is the first
comprehensive introduction to the thought
of Elisée Reclus, the great anarchist geographer and political theorist.
It shows him to be an extraordinary figure for his age. Not only an
anarchist but also a radical feminist, anti-racist, ecologist, animal rights
advocate, cultural radical, nudist, and vegetarian. Not only a major social
thinker but also a dedicated revolutionary.

The work analyzes Reclus' greatest achievement, a sweeping historical
and theoretical synthesis recounting the story of the earth and
humanity as an epochal struggle between freedom and domination. It
presents his groundbreaking critique of all forms of domination: not
only capitalism, the state, and authoritarian religion, but also patriarchy,
racism, technological domination, and the domination of nature. His
crucial insights on the interrelation between personal and small-
group transformation, broader cultural change, and large-scale social
organization are explored. Reclus' ideas are presented both through
detailed exposition and analysis, and in extensive translations of key
texts, most appearing in English for the first time.

*"For far too long Elisée Reclus has stood in the shadow of Godwin, Proudhon,
Bakunin, Kropotkin, and Emma Goldman. Now John Clark has pulled Reclus
forward to stand shoulder to shoulder with Anarchism's cynosures. Reclus'
light brought into anarchism's compass not only a focus on ecology, but a
struggle against both patriarchy and racism, contributions which can now
be fully appreciated thanks to John Clark's exegesis and [his and Camille
Martin's] translations of works previously unavailable in English. No serious
reader can afford to neglect this book."*
—Dana Ward, Pitzer College

*"Finally! A century after his death, the great French geographer and anarchist
Elisée Reclus has been honored by a vibrant selection of his writings expertly
translated into English."*
—Kent Mathewson, Louisiana State University

Voices of the Paris Commune

Edited by Mitchell Abidor

ISBN: 978-1-62963-100-4
$14.95   128 pages

The Paris Commune of 1871, the first instance of a working-class seizure of power, has been subject to countless interpretations; reviled by its enemies as a murderous bacchanalia of the unwashed while praised by supporters as an exemplar of proletarian anarchism in action. As both a successful model to be imitated and as a devastating failure to be avoided. All of the interpretations are tendentious. Historians view the working class's three-month rule through their own prism, distant in time and space. *Voices of the Paris Commune* takes a different tack. In this book only those who were present in the spring of 1871, who lived through and participated in the Commune, are heard.

The Paris Commune had a vibrant press, and it is represented here by its most important newspaper, *Le Cri du Peuple*, edited by Jules Vallès, member of the First International. Like any legitimate government, the Paris Commune held parliamentary sessions and issued daily printed reports of the heated, contentious deliberations that belie any accusation of dictatorship. Included in this collection is the transcript of the debate in the Commune, just days before its final defeat, on the establishing of a Committee of Public Safety and on the fate of the hostages held by the Commune, hostages who would ultimately be killed.

Finally, *Voices of the Paris Commune* contains a selection from the inquiry carried out twenty years after the event by the intellectual review *La Revue Blanche*, asking participants to judge the successes and failures of the Paris Commune. This section provides a fascinating range of opinions of this epochal event.

"The Paris Commune of 1871 has been the subject of much ideological debate, often far removed from the experiences of the participants themselves. If you really want to dig deep into what happened during those fateful weeks, reading these eyewitness accounts is mandatory."
—Gabriel Kuhn, editor of *All Power to the Councils! A Documentary History of the German Revolution of 1918-1919*

The Great French Revolution, 1789–1793

Peter Kropotkin
with an Introduction by David Berry

ISBN: 978-1-62963-876-8
$29.95   448 pages

The Great French Revolution, 1789–1793 is
Peter Kropotkin's most substantial historical
work. In it he presents a people's history of
the world-shaking events of the Revolution and shows the key role the
working men and women of the towns and countryside played in it.
Without the constant pressure of popular organisations and activity, the
politicians would never have created a Republic, nor been able to survive
the counterrevolutionary forces internally or externally.

Focusing on such mass movements—and especially the peasant
majority—rather than on the few great men beloved of bourgeois
accounts, this is a groundbreaking account of the period and a seminal
work of "history from below." Later research may have corrected some
factual details and opened new avenues of scholarship, but Kropotkin's
text remains an exemplar of anarchist history-writing, challenging both
bourgeois republican and Marxist interpretations of the Revolution.

Yet it is more than a history: Kropotkin uses the experience of the French
Revolution to aid us in our current struggles and to learn its lessons in
order to ensure the success of future revolutions. This book raises issues
which have resurfaced time and again, as well as offering solutions
based on the self-activity of the masses, the new, decentralised, directly
democratic social organisations they forged during the Revolution, and
the need to transform a political revolt into a social revolution which seeks
to secure the well-being of all by transforming the economy from the start.

"*The French Revolution erupted out of the remnants of the old world and
set a dynamic precedent for new centuries of resistance. Multifaceted,
contradictory, and compelling, the French Revolution cast an enormous
shadow that influenced every radical faction of 19th century politics. Peter
Kropotkin was perhaps the preeminent anarchist intellect of his generation,
and so his book* The Great French Revolution, 1789–1793 *provides us
with a fascinating exploration into the late 19th century anarchist vision
of historical transformation. This saga of popular upheaval from below
provides a fascinating mirror image of how Kropotkin and many of his
comrades envisioned the coming revolution.*"
—Mark Bray, author of *Antifa: The Anti-Fascist Handbook* and co-editor of
Anarchist Education and the Modern School: A Francisco Ferrer Reader